Real and Financial Dynamics
in a Macroeconomic Growth Model
with Endogenous Cycles

Dynamische Wirtschaftstheorie
Dynamic Economic Theory

Edited by/Herausgegeben von Carl Chiarella, Peter Flaschel, Reiner Franke, Michael Krüger, Ingrid Kubin, Thomas Lux, Willi Semmler, Peter Skott

Vol./Bd. 20

PETER LANG
Frankfurt am Main · Berlin · Bern · New York · Paris · Wien

Eleonora Cavallaro

Real and Financial Dynamics in a Macroeconomic Growth Model with Endogenous Cycles

PETER LANG
Europäischer Verlag der Wissenschaften

Die Deutsche Bibliothek - CIP-Einheitsaufnahme

Cavallaro, Eleonora:

Real and Financial Dynamics in a Macroeconomic Growth Model with Endogenous Cycles / Eleonora Cavallaro. - Frankfurt am Main ; Berlin ; Bern ; New York ; Paris ; Wien : Lang, 1999
(Dynamische Wirtschaftstheorie ; Bd. 20)
Zugl.: Rom, Univ. "La Sapienza", Diss., 1998
ISBN 3-631-35033-3

ISSN 0930-2174
ISBN 3-631-35033-3
US-ISBN 0-8204-4345-X

PREFACE TO THE SERIES

With the series "Dynamische Wirtschaftstheorie" the editors intend to encourage and support contributions to dynamic macro- and micro-economic analysis. The main fields of publications should cover work on business and growth cycle theories, stability of market systems, new directions in dynamic economic theory, and applications of new methods to theoretical as well as empirical problems of economic dynamics.

Conditions for the publication of dissertations can be obtained on request from the editors. Manuscripts - no less than 100 and no more than 400 pages in length - should be sent to:

Prof. Dr. Peter Flaschel
Universität Bielefeld
Fakultät für Wirtschaftswissenschaften
Postfach 100 131
D-33501 Bielefeld
West Germany

TABLE OF CONTENTS

INTRODUCTION

One of the most challenging tasks in economics is understanding the mechanisms that govern the dynamic processes in modern capitalist economies. Over the years, economists have addressed this issue, developing complex and refined methods for theoretical analysis and empirical investigation.

In fact, except for the Sixties, studies on business cycles have faithfully accompanied history of economic thought, searching for insights into the factors determining the recurrent expansions and contractions of economic activity which, at times, lead to instability and crises.

In most of the earlier literature the prevailing attitude was towards a separate study of the two phenomena of economic dynamics – that is, business cycles and growth. Yet, this point of view obliterates the links between short-run periodic movements and long-run tendencies which, indeed, raise numerous and complex analytical problems. Given the analytical complexities in explaining the processes through which short-run dynamics contribute to the determination of the trend itself, most authors assume that the trend is determined exogenously by the growth rates of technical progress and population.

Early attempts at a rigorous analysis of business cycles were made during the Thirties, in the so-called "contemporary" stage of business cycle theory. At the end of the nineteenth century, however, some authors had already come up with some intuitive interpretations of economic fluctuations, but without succeeding in elaborating a rigorous model. Some of the most famous are, for instance, Juglar, Jevons and Tugar-Baranovskij, forerunners of the so-called "modern" stage of business cycle theory, and later Hawtrey, Hayek, Wicksell and Schumpeter. Explanations for business cycles were attributed, in the two different cases, to real factors and to monetary factors, respectively. These earlier contributors were then joined by the so-called "underconsumption" theorists, in particular Hobson, who emphasised the role of demand - rather than supply - factors in the analysis of economic fluctuations.

Keynes's theoretical revolution (1936), and in particular the subsequent developments of the analysis, paved the way for the "contemporary" stage of business cycle theory. Keynes's basic idea was that fluctuations constitute the "shape" itself or the "pattern" of the dynamic processes in modern capitalist economies, and are not the result of the interference of the banking system on *real* equilibrium, as in Hayek's perspective. This argument was explained with the well known proposition that there is no automatic mechanism in the economic system which makes investment and saving decisions consistent over time, in spite of the presence of a "neutral" banking system. For the economic process takes place, fundamentally, within real time, and agents form expectations under uncertainty conditions, thus causing the instability of the "marginal efficiency" of capital. All this ultimately affects the accumulation process and the overall macroeconomic dynamics.

The Keynesian tradition in the macrodynamic modelling of business cycles started with the works of Harrod (1939, 1948) and Domar (1946, 1957), who first highlighted the issues of the instability of equilibrium in a growth model. After the works of these authors and, particularly, building on the subsequent contributions by Samuelson (1939), and Hicks (1950), there followed a very successful generation of models based on the multiplier-accelerator interaction and on the utilisation of lags in behavioural functions. This model building was the dominant reference especially during the Fifties and the Sixties, and its distinguishing features are the explanation of income fluctuations on the basis of demand side factors, the assumption of constant prices and the restriction of the analysis to *real* factors alone.

A fundamental place in the debate on the cyclical behaviour of economic systems is held by Kalecki's influential contribution (1935 and onwards). The author shares Keynes's theoretical "view" as to the belief that fluctuations constitute the most typical feature of the - inherently endogenous - dynamics of capitalist systems.

Two different fundamental approaches characterise recent contemporary literature, one being of the Neo-Classical school, the other of the Keynesian tradition.

As is well known, the *Neo-Classical synthesis* has given a positive answer to the question raised by Keynes in the General Theory regarding the *invisible hand*'s ability to accomplish the full utilisation of resources at the macroeconomic level, thus co-ordinating agents' behaviour in each market and between markets. Within that theoretical setting, the Keynesian results and prescriptions are applied to special cases - specifically regarding the short run - of an overall dynamic process which fundamentally tends to stable growth thanks to the existence of endogenous self-correcting mechanisms.

In spite of the presence of "institutions" which, in the "real world", might interfere with the spontaneous working of markets, thus slowing down the aforesaid stabilising effects, the self-correcting mechanism is never compromised. Besides, money and financial factors appear to be neutral in equilibrium, although they might cause interference off the equilibrium position. In any case, the system eventually approaches the full utilisation of resources by removing the rigidities that contrast the adjustment to equilibrium, and by absorbing the shocks that cause the departure from the steady-state position.

There is a long tradition in macrodynamic literature that shares this view that economic systems, fundamentally stable at the stationary equilibrium, might experience casual but transitory perturbations that are responsible for the cyclical behaviour evident in macroeconomic variables. This view, common to most recent business cycle models of the Neo-Classical approach, goes back to the works of Slutsky (1927) and Frisch (1933), in which fluctuations are the result of the economic system's reactions to the continuous *exogenous* shocks.

In the so-called *Equilibrium Business Cycle* models of the more recent New Classical literature, the aforementioned shocks may concern monetary aggregates – as in the *monetary* theory by Lucas (1981) – or real variables such as technology or consumer preferences – as in the *real* theories of the cycle by Kydland and Prescott (1982) and Long and Plosser (1983).

According to the New Classical approach fluctuations are phenomena which are consistent with the assumptions of perfect markets and rational behaviour of agents. Were financial variables always *neutral* in relation to the economic performance, then, the dynamics of a system not affected by external shocks could be explained perfectly and defined by real variables alone. This statement is based on the strong assumptions of market-clearing and rational expectations, on which the *equilibrium* models are built, and on a rather simplified and stylised view of the working of economic systems. In particular, all the complexities deriving from the existence of sophisticated financial structures in the "real world" are completely ignored, and markets are assumed to be always perfect co-ordinators of investment and saving decisions.

The New Keynesian approach actually builds on these criticisms of the New Classical methodological approach[1]. New Keynesians focus their attention on the working of goods, labour and financial markets in the presence of *sticky prices* – that is, price rigidities – with a view to understanding the impulse-propagation mechanism which is responsible for the recurrent contractions and expansions of economic activity, notwithstanding agents' optimizing behaviour.

---

1 In this regard, see L. H. Summers (1986); N. G. Mankiw (1989). For a review of the New Keynesian approach cf., among others, N. G. Mankiw – D. Romer (1991).

Indeed, since within that theoretical setting unemployment and recession occur as a result of agents' optimizing behaviour, they are ultimately explained by endogenous factors[2].

The "active" role of *financial* variables in the explanation of fluctuations constitutes the distinctive feature of another recent approach to business cycle theory. This new field of research moves in the direction of the Post-Keynesian research programme, building on the *debt-deflation* school of thought and Minsky's theoretical contribution (1975). Among some very interesting developments in this field of research are the contributions which aim to take account of the New Keynesian analyses in microeconomics, particularly with regard to the theory of financial markets.

Common to both strands of research in the Keynesian approach is the idea that fluctuations constitute the very way market forces are at work in the presence of uncertainty and co-ordination failures, which are a typical feature of developed capitalist economies. Within this theoretical context, the financial structure as a whole, that is the set of all markets and intermediaries, represents the response of the economic system to the above problems; hence, it is endogenous and interacts with the *real* side of the economy, thus intimately affecting its behaviour.

Yet, one distinctive feature of the New Keynesian theoretical view is the belief that fluctuations are essentially due to imperfections in financial markets, which act as a propagation mechanism of the – *real* or *monetary* – disturbances in the economic process[3]. In the Post Keynesian perspective, on the other hand, instability is considered a systemic, and hence unavoidable, characteristic of economic systems with sophisticated, and yet intrinsically fragile, financial

---

2 See the comment in M. Dore (1993), p. 6.

3 These aspects are discussed in R. J. Gordon (1986) – Introduction.

structures. It is, therefore, necessary to single out the "endogenous mechanisms" which drive the economic process, and which generate fluctuations and instability.

This task may be achieved by means of the theoretical schemes of non-linear dynamics, following the seminal works on *endogenous* business cycle theory by Kaldor (1940), Goodwin (1948, 1951) and Kalecki (1971)[4]. And yet, in those contributions *monetary* factors have no essential role in driving the cycle, a role which Wicksell and Schumpeter had strongly emphasized, even before Keynes.

The present work draws, fundamentally, on this endogenous approach to the analysis of economic fluctuations, and follows some typical features of the Keynesian macrodynamic modelling. The starting point of the work is a close examination of the main models in the literature. More specifically, some theoretical models have emphasised the role of *real* determinants of business cycles, due to either the dynamic interaction of income distribution and the employment rate, or to various kinds of multiplier-accelerator processes; other models have drawn attention to the role of *financial* factors, essentially focusing on the dynamics of debt, and its effects on *financial fragility* and *systemic risk*.

Building on some basic mechanisms highlighted in the literature, the work proceeds with an analysis of economic fluctuations which is presented in two stages. The starting point is the development of a model in which the dynamics is fundamentally driven by *real* factors; the basic set up is then extended to allow for the interaction of *financial* and *real* factors in the cyclical process.

The work is organised as follows. The first two Chapters are introductory to the central part of the work and, in particular, Chapter I looks at the main

---

4 Collected studies on financial fragility and the role of financial determinants of business cycles are in the volumes edited by W. Semmler (1989) and (1994).

“stylized facts” of the dynamics of developed capitalist economies, whereas Chapter II reviews some of the “reference” models in endogenous business cycle theory. Chapter III introduces a basic set up for a growth cycle model, in which the monetary sector is treated in a very simplified way. Chapter IV then extends the analysis in order to introduce the issue of firms’ indebtedness and the associated liquidity creation process by the banking system.

Both Chapters III and IV start with an analysis of the short-run characteristics of the models, in the form of a traditional IS-LM framework for the basic set up (model I), and of an “enlarged” IS-LM scheme for the following extension (model II). Both models have a typical Keynesian structure: in particular, with a given monetary wage in the short run and prices determined on the basis of a *mark-up* function over costs, the real wage is determined in the goods market. Following Kalecki, it is assumed that workers consume all their income, in the form of wages, whereas capitalists (*rentiers*) save part of the profits accruing from firms. The latter make their investment decisions in view of the difference between the expected rate of profit and the real interest rate. As to the monetary sector, the analysis of model II becomes more articulated because of the broader concept of money, which is made endogenous by considering the liquidity created by the bank financing of firms.

In the last section of each Chapter, then, the long-run characteristics and the dynamic properties of both the basic and the extended models are discussed. In the first case, emphasis is placed on the role of *real* factors in the cyclical behaviour of the economy, which manifest themselves essentially through the impact of the market structure on firms’ pricing strategies and on the dynamics of income distribution. In the second case, the stress is on the way that *financial* factors interact with the aforementioned *real* factors, in particular through the impact of the liquidity creation process on the dynamics of debt, thus affecting the overall macroeconomic behaviour of the system in time.

Here is a short summary of the basic assumptions and results of the work.

To begin with, following an assumption common to the Keynesian tradition in the macrodynamic modelling of business cycles, it is assumed that the growth rate of money wages is governed by the law implicit in the Phillips curve.

As to income distribution, assuming competition is not perfect in markets, its behaviour is made to depend on firms' pricing strategies, given the variations in the "direct costs" over time - that is, wages and productivity. This argument stems from the observation that each firm aims to keep the market-share of its own product constant in the presence of uncertainty as to the demand and the strategies of the other firms – which is a typical feature of imperfectly competitive settings. According to Sylos-Labini (1967), this consideration would take account of the fact that, over time, variations in prices appear to be less than proportional with respect to variations in "direct costs".

Apart from this determinant of price variations, an additional component is introduced which captures the "direct" effect of the demand pressure on price changes over time. This "direct" effect is signalled by the behaviour of real liquidity in the system, which is thus assumed to act as an indicator of the purchasing power and hence to reflect the performance of the "state of demand". Therefore, the behaviour of firms' margins over time, and consequently the dynamics of income-shares, depends on the resultant of both components of price variations: the first effect brings about a reduction in the profit-share in expansionary periods, whereas the second effect induces firms to regain their profit margins during periods of high liquidity, and hence a good "state of demand", and vice versa in periods of low liquidity and stagnant demand, thus working in the opposite direction to the first effect.

Finally, it is assumed that expectations over investment profitability, which represent the "state of confidence" of firms, are directly correlated with the level of aggregate demand, and thus with the rate of capacity utilisation.

In steady-state equilibrium the system grows at a rate equal to the sum of the growth rates of the labour force and productivity, with a constant income distribution between profits and wages and with money growing at a rate equal to the sum of the growth rates of prices and the capital stock.

The behaviour of the system out of equilibrium is explained by the dynamic equations of the model. Under the assumptions of model I, the system is essentially governed by *real* factors. Basically, the mechanism at work is the following. Firms' strategies as to the *mark-up* over costs depend on the level of aggregate demand and the associated capacity utilisation rate over time, given the degree of competition in the market. More specifically, "direct costs" move pro-cyclically and the market structure influences the sensitivity of price changes to variations in costs, thus determining the behaviour of firms' *mark-up* over time and, consequently, the dynamics of income distribution. In particular, the lower the degree of competition in the market, the higher each firm's uncertainty about its rivals' strategies, and consequently, the greater the concern for its own market-share, which induces a higher degree of *inertia* in the adjustment of prices to the changes occurring in costs over time. All this ultimately affects the dynamics of income distribution during the cycle, which in turn feeds back to the performance of aggregate demand and to the associated rate of capacity utilisation over the cycle. The parameters in the equations corresponding to the laws of motion of prices and of the firms' margins are crucial since they determine the dynamics of income distribution over time. Ultimately, they influence the overall behaviour of the model and the stability properties.

Under the assumptions of model II the behaviour of the system is affected by *financial* factors, which are specifically linked to the dynamics of debt, as emphasised by that strand of the literature that combines the *financial fragility* hypothesis *à la* Minsky with the New Keynesian developments on financial markets. According to that literature, the well-known information problems which occur in the concrete working of credit markets might amplify the negative effects resulting from firms' deteriorated financial structures due to excess debt. Within that context, the financial structure of firms acts as an indicator of their default-risk, thus affecting the availability of finance for the accumulation process. It may happen that increasing levels of indebtedness, which typically characterise the late stage of an expansion, heighten the degree of financial fragility, thus leading to contractions in the overall liquidity which may foster instability.

Finally, the main results of the work are given and some closing remarks are made in the Conclusions.

Two Appendixes follow and close the work. Appendix A contains some formal demonstrations related to the models surveyed in Chapter II, with explanatory notes on dynamic systems and their use in economic analysis. Appendix B contains a detailed analysis of the models developed in Chapters III and IV, with a discussion of the dynamic properties using the tools of bifurcation analysis and giving a simple numerical illustration.

✧ ✧ ✧ ✧ ✧

The present work is the English version of my doctoral dissertation, which I elaborated at the Faculty of Economics of the University of Rome "La Sapienza". The thesis was completed in February 1998, submitted and accepted in June 1998. It was then translated into English in the Autumn of the same year, with minor changes to the original manuscript and with a different subdivision of Chapters and Sections.

I wish to thank my thesis supervisor Professor Ferruccio Marzano for helpful discussion and stimulating comments, and for constant encouragement during my research work. I am also grateful to Dr. Michele Tucci, with whom I discussed various parts of the work and, in particular, formal aspects of the analysis. And finally, I would like to thank Professor Peter Flaschel for having read the manuscript and made the publication in this *Series* possible.

CHAPTER I

The “Stylized Facts” in the Dynamics of Capitalist Economies

“Analyzing business cycles means nothing more nor less than analyzing the economic process of the capitalist era”[1].

According to Schumpeter, economic fluctuations represent the “shape” itself of the economic process in modern capitalist economies, and not “*separable things that may be treated by themselves*”. Fluctuations represent, indeed, the intrinsic characteristic of the growth process of modern capitalist economies.

Distinctive features of business cycles are two phenomena which are drawn from the observation of the behaviour of macroeconomic variables: “persistence” – that is, the tendency of the level of a variable to fluctuate in the same direction for more than one period – and “co-movements” among variables. In fact, theoretical studies and empirical investigations have long been focusing precisely on these two aspects.

In an analysis of the behaviour of an economic system and the laws that govern its dynamic processes attention is generally drawn to a limited number of variables, and a certain degree of abstraction and simplification is, thus, unavoidable. In fact, a theoretical model aims fundamentally to seek the key variables, and to explain their relationship to each others and the mechanisms that lead to the turning points in the cyclical process. In other words, it aims to provide an analytical framework within which the laws behind the “stylised facts” obtained from the empirical evidence can be interpreted. For this reason,

1 J. A. Schumpeter (1939), p. 5.

the "stylised facts" represent a necessary starting point in the analysis of business cycles.

A quick overview of the empirical patterns of the most fundamental variables in developed capitalist economies is presented in this Chapter.

As is well known, the National Bureau of Economic Research has a long tradition in the study of business cycles, particularly with respect to the collection of data and the development of indicators for measuring and forecasting cycles. The works by the NBER, which mainly refer to the American economy, are nonetheless of general interest and a constant reference for similar studies regarding other countries.

An important introduction in the study of the stylised facts of business cycles is the seminal work by Wesley Mitchell (1927), and his later contribution with Arthur Burns (1946). The following definition of business cycles given by the authors is still nowadays the one most commonly found in use in the literature and adopted by the NBER itself:

"Business cycles are a type of fluctuation in the aggregate activity of nations that organize their work mainly in business enterprises: a cycle consists of expansions occurring at about the same time in many economic activities, followed by similarly general recessions, contractions, and revivals which merge into the expansion phase of the next cycle; this sequence of changes is recurrent but not periodic; in duration business cycles vary from more than one year to ten or twelve years; they are not divisible into shorter cycles of similar character with amplitudes approximating their own"[2].

In fact, authors and students of different schools and theoretical approaches seem to agree upon the above definition.

---

2 A. Burns – W. Mitchell (1946), p. 3.

To begin with, periodic movements were observed of different length and intensity with the specific features emphasized in each case and with the associated dynamic relations. According to Schumpeter's (1939) classification, it is possible to identify at least three different types of cyclical waves, on the basis of the observed regularities[3]. There are the long waves studied by Kondratieff, of approximately forty to fifty years length, detected by observing the consumption of iron in Germany and Great Britain. Cyclical movements of this kind could be explained by the major structural changes of the modern capitalist era due to "revolutionary" technological innovations, particularly steam-power, railways and electricity, and appear to be associated with large scale movements in prices. Given the limited availability of data, only three cycles of these kind were detected.

From the observation of price and interest rate movements in France, Great Britain and the United States, cycles of approximately seven to eleven years length were detected, which correspond more or less to the life of investment goods. This kind of cycle is characterised by fluctuations in output, employment and the inflation rate, and constitutes the middle-length waves studied by Juglar.

Finally, shorter waves, of no more than four years length, were detected by Kitchin while observing the behaviour of bank clearings and whole-sale prices in Great Britain and France. In this case, fluctuations are determined by casual shocks, which have an immediate effect on the inventory stocks of firms, and may lead to a temporary deviation of variables such as output, employment and the inflation rate from their equilibrium values.

---

3 Indeed, other kinds of cycles have been considered in the literature, too. It is possible to find some empirical evidence for the Kutznetz cycles, of approximately fifteen to twenty-five years length, which emerge in correspondence to factors such as the growth of population and labour force, the development of cities and transportation.

The Juglar-type waves, to which the Burns and Mitchell definition apply, are the middle-length movements considered in the present work. Over time, in modern economies their duration has shortened to periods of four to seven years. Besides, this is the kind of cyclical movement which V. Zarnovitz and G. Moore also refer to. In their well known work (1986), the history and the role of the NBER's chronologies on business cycles are presented with time-series and tables that cover a period of three centuries. Their study outlines the evolution in the cyclical behaviour of the United States in the given period of time, with a view to highlighting the major changes which have taken place in the behaviour of the most important macroeconomic aggregates, as well as in the length, frequency and severity of business cycles.

Some of the most interesting features that emerge from the contribution by Zarnovitz and Moore are briefly reviewed below, given their usefulness in describing the changes which have occurred in the leading developed capitalist economies. This will help in sketching the "stylized facts" of business cycles and in outlining the changes that these patterns have undergone over time.

Briefly, the following features emerge. First of all, the relationship between growth and cyclical movements in business activity; secondly, the existence of an upward trend in the relative length of expansions with respect to contractions (this pattern is associated with the changes in the trend of prices, which is another factor investigated in the work); and thirdly, the decreasing severity of recessions after the Great Depression. In the authors' opinion, this is due to structural determinants such as a change in the composition of the labour force, a variation in the level of unemployment and participation in the labour force or the role of government intervention through demand management and distributive policies.

To begin with, the NBER chronologies reveal a secular tendency towards growth in capitalist systems, as is made evident from the long-run trends in the growth rates of output, capital, productivity, employment and per-capita consumption.

This long-run general tendency may be broken down into sub-periods characterised by *"recurrent sequences of persistent and pervasive expansions and contractions in economic activities"*[4], which constitute cycles in the true sense of the word. Therefore, growth is the result of oscillatory cyclical movements in which each period (cycle) is generally distinguished by a peak which is higher than the one of the previous period, and similarly, by a trough which is not so low as the preceding one, so that altogether the contraction following an expansion does not completely cancel out the gains in economic activity. Hence, the result is net positive growth.

Moore-Zarnovitz (1986) illustrates the reference dates - showing the peaks and troughs - and the duration of business cycles in two tables. The first table refers to Great Britain and the United States with annual data covering the period 1790-1858, whereas the second refers to the United States, France, Germany and Great Britain with monthly, quarterly and annual data up to 1938. Both tables reveal a close conformity between cycles in the four different countries, a correspondence which is further enhanced in periods of financial crises and instability, that is, in the years 1815, 1825, 1836, 1847, 1857, 1873, 1893, 1907 and 1929.

A summary of the (detailed) information given in those records is presented in the following Table (1.1) and Table (1.2). Altogether, fourteen cycles can be detected in the first period (1790-1858), averaging about four years and a half in duration, whereas in the following period (up to 1938) a higher number of cycles is observed, which tend to be shorter in length for the United States, followed by France, Great Britain and Germany.

---

4 V. Zarnovitz – G. Moore (1986), p. 520.

The number of cycles and the corresponding durations for the period 1879-1938 in the four countries are then shown in Summary (I), which follows Table (1.1) and Table (1.2). The characteristics of the last period observed, up to 1982, are illustrated in Table (1.3), which refers only to the United States.

Table 1.1 : Duration of Business Cycle, 1790-1858

	Duration in Years *(Averages)*			
	Contraction *(P to T)*	Expansion *(T to P)*	Full Cycle *(T to T)*	Full Cycle *(P to P)*
(A) Great Britain				
Mean duration (years)	1.3	3.3	4.3	4.6
Standard deviation (years)	0.7	1.5	1.5	1.8
Mean duration (years)	1.3	3.3	4.3	4.6
Standard deviation (years)	0.7	1.5	1.5	1.8
(B) United States				
Mean duration (years)	2.0	2.6	4.6	4.4
Standard deviation (years)	1.5	1.5	2.4	1.6

P= Peak; T= Trough .

Source: G. Moore - V. Zarnovitz (1986), Table A.2, p. 746.

Table 1.2 : Business Cycle Durations to 1938

(A) United States, 1854-1938

	Duration in Months *(Averages)*			
	Contraction	Expansion	Full Cycle	
	(P to T)	*(T to P)*	*(T to T)*	*(P to P)*
Twenty-one cycles, 1854-1938				
Mean duration (months)	21	26	48	48
Standard deviation (months)	14	11	18	20
Thirty-five cycles, 1790-1938				
Mean duration (months)	23	28	50	50
Standard deviation (months)	16	14	24	20

(B) Great Britain, 1854-1938

	Duration in months *(Averages)*			
	Contraction	Expansion	Full Cycle	
	(P to T)	*(T to P)*	*(T to T)*	*(P to P)*
Sixteen cycles, 1854-1938				
Mean duration (months)	26	37	63	64
Standard deviation (months)	19	18	29	33
Twenty-nine cycles, 1790-1938				
Mean duration (months)	22	39	60	62
Standard deviation (months)	16	18	24	28

(continued)

(continued)

(C) France, 1865-1938

	Duration in Months *(Averages)*			
	Contraction	Expansion	Full Cycle	
	(P to T)	*(T to P)*	*(T to T)*	*(P to P)*
Mean duration (months)	22	29	51	52
Standard deviation (months)	16	15	23	25

(D) Germany, 1879-1932

	Duration in Months *(Averages)*			
	Contraction	Expansion	Full Cycle	
	(P to T)	*(T to P)*	*(T to T)*	*(P to P)*
Mean duration (months)	27	37	64	63
Standard deviation (months)	18	14	24	29

P= Peak; T= Trough.

Source: G. Moore - V. Zarnovitz (1986), Table A.3, pp. 750-753.

Summary (I)

	United States	Great Britain	France	Germany
N° of cycles *(trough to trough)*	17	13	14	10
Mean duration *(months)*	48	65	53	64

Source: G. Moore - V. Zarnovitz (1986), p. 754.

In the last period under scrutiny there are ten cycles, lasting on average a little more than four years. The interesting feature is the average duration of contractions and expansions over the whole period (Table 1.3). In fact, at the beginning it appears to be approximately the same in the two phases, whereas later expansions last much longer than contractions, even up to four times longer after the Great Depression, as shown in Summary (II), which follows Table 1.3.

Table 1.3 : Business Cycle Durations to 1982
United States

	Duration in Months			
	Contraction	Expansion	Full Cycle	
	(P to T)	*(T to P)*	*(T to T)*	*(P to P)*
	Averages			
Ten cycles, 1933-1982				
Mean duration (months)	11	49	60	59
Standard deviation (months)	3	27	26	31
Thirty cycles, 1884-1982				
Mean duration (months)	18	33	51	50
Standard deviation (months)	12	20	21	23
Forty-four cycles, 1790-1982				
Mean duration (months)	20	33	52	51
Standard deviation (months)	15	20	24	22

Source: G. Moore - V. Zarnovitz (1986), Table A.5, p. 765.

Furthermore, contractions prove to be much more uniform in length, and thus more predictable. This is signalled by the standard deviation (Table 1.3), which has fallen considerably over time, whereas the opposite has happened for expansions.

Summary (II)

	1834-55	1857-82	1885-99	1900-1918	1919-37	1948-82
N° of cycles	5	5	5	5	5	8
Expansions *(months)*	26	31	22	26	26	45
Contractions *(months)*	24	28	19	20	19	11
Ratio Exp./Contr.	1.1	1.1	1.2	1.3	1.4	4.1
Source: G. Moore - V. Zarnovitz (1986), p. 755.						

Moreover, since the Great Depression recessions have become less severe, and there has been increased stability over time. Zarnovitz and Moore stress how this tendency is connected with the rising trend in prices. In fact, it may be noticed that prolonged expansions in relation to contractions are associated with a rising trend in prices, and vice-versa, and this may be explained by the greater upward pressure onto prices during business expansions. This point is illustrated in Table (1.4).

As far as the behaviour of prices is concerned, in the hundred-and-fifty years before the Great Depression upward and downward trends alternated, though in the end they balanced each other out. In fact, the price level at the trough of the Great Depression was more or less the same as the one prevailing at the end of the eighteenth century. Instead, starting from 1932 and right up to

1982, there was a process of rising prices of huge dimensions, and inflation became a structural problem of developed economies.

Table. 1.4 : Trend in Wholesale Prices and Relative Duration of Business Cycle Expansions and Contractions (1790-1982)

Trend in Prices	Expansions		Contractions		Ratio
	N°	Duration [A] months*	N°	Duration [B] months*	Exp./Contr. [A/B]
		United States			
Rising					
1789-1814	5	42	4	22	1.9
1843-64	6	32	5	15	2.1
1896-1920	7	23	6	18	1.3
1932-82	10	43	10	11	4.5
Total or Average	28	36	25	16	2.2
Falling					
1814-43	6	27	7	27	1.0
1864-96	7	25	8	26	1.0
1920-32	3	23	4	22	1.0
Total or Average	16	25	19	25	1.0
		Great Britain			
Rising					
1854-73, 1896-1920	10	38	8	17	2.2
Falling					
1873-96, 1920-33	5	30	7	38	0.8

(continued)

(continued)					
		France			
Rising					
1865-73, 1896-1926	11	31	9	15	2.1
Falling					
1873-96, 1926-35	4	30	6	34	0.9
		Germany			
Rising					
1895-1923	6	40	6	18	2.2
Falling					
1923-33	4	32	4	42	0.8
* = *averages.*					
Source: V. Zarnovitz - G. Moore (1986), Table 9.3, p. 528.					

All this may be explained by the fact that, although the short-run price indexes show prevalently a pro-cyclical behaviour, after the Second World War capitalist economies experienced stagflationary processes for the first time, that is, the simultaneous contraction of economic activity and rise in price inflation. Practically, price increases were not cancelled out by contractions, and there was no inversion in the growth rate of prices, as shown from Table (1.5).

It is only more recently that this vicious inflationary tendency seems to have come under control in most developed countries. This could be explained on the one hand by a growing reluctance to resort to high budget deficits and therefore a more limited use of demand management policies which are considered too inflationary; and on the other hand by the concomitant widespread slowdown in business activity in most European countries, starting in the late Eighties and continuing throughout the Nineties, which has also turned into a severe recession in some countries, as for instance in the Far East, where recovery does not seem to have started up yet.

Table 1.5: Long-Term Trends and Average Cyclical Changes in Prices, United States, 1789-1982

Trend in Wholesale Prices *(WPI)*			Average % Change in WPI (annual rate)	
Direction	Dates	Number of Years	Expansions	Contractions
Rising	1789-1814	25		
Falling	1814-43	29		
Rising	1843-64	21		
Falling	1864-96	32	0.4	-2.3
Rising	1896-1920	24	9.7	-1.6
Falling	1920-32	12	2.1	-13.7
Rising	1932-82	50	6.5	1.8
Total or average		193		

Source: V. Zarnovitz - G. Moore (1986), Table. 9.2, p. 527.

As for the behaviour of interest rates, there appears to be a close relationship between interest rates, especially short-term rates, and the performance of the economy during the cycle, given the high sensitivity of financial markets to any event which might affect the "state of affairs". In the post-World War II period, and until the 1980s, there was a general upward trend in interest rates, in particular after the Sixties, mostly as a reflection of the higher rates of inflation and their effects on expectations. And moreover, this period showed an increased volatility during cycles, as is evident from the comparison of the graphs in Figure (1).

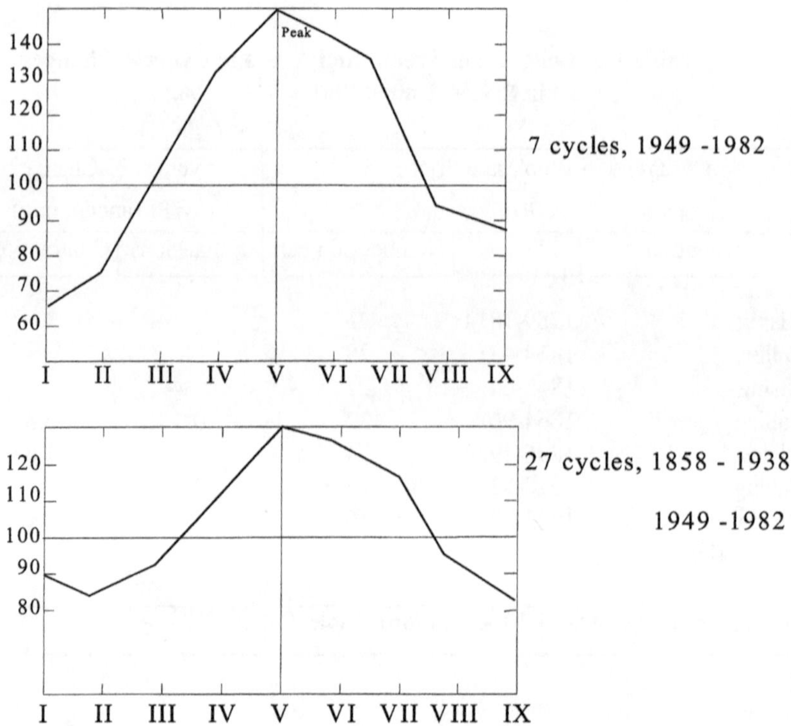

Source: V. Zarnovitz – G. Moore (1986), Fig. 9.2, p. 563.

Fig.1. *U.S. Treasury bill rates, average reference patterns, 1858-1982*

Here the average reference pattern of short-run interest rates on American Treasury Bills is divided into nine phases, each lasting three months. On the abscissae of the graph, phase I corresponds to the initial trough, phase V to the peak and phase IX to the final trough. Phases II, III and IV cover the period of expansion, whereas phases VI, VII and VIII the period of contraction.

This upward trend in interest rates was inverted with the recent general slowdown of economic activity and the end of the strong inflationary pressures of the Seventies.

As far as long-term interest rates are concerned, they appear to be less volatile with respect to the short-term rates, and their behaviour does not follow as closely the cycle. In particular, they seem to fall for a good part of the recovery following a recession. The short-run pattern is characterised by a more evident amplitude of oscillations and, notably, by a strong upward trend in the last period.

It was mentioned above that, after the Great Depression, structural factors have helped to mitigate the effects of a recession. Moore and Zarnovitz confirm this tendency by using an indicator built with data on the GNP, industrial production, non-farm employment and employment rate, to evaluate the patterns of duration, depth and diffusion of contractions in the United States.

Another very important issue in the analysis of business cycles is the frequency of the risk of financial crises caused by the structural instability of modern capitalist economies with sophisticated, yet fragile, financial structures. Research on this topic has drawn considerably on the empirical evidence of the behaviour of financial variables over the cycle, in particular firms' financial ratios which constitute the main indicators of their financial equilibrium and default-risk.

Table (1.6) shows the behaviour of some leverage indicators for non-financial firms in the United States during the cycle, in the period 1953-1981. These records confirm the close relationship between financial fragility and economic performance.

Table 1.6 : Average Values of Various Leverage Ratios for U.S Nonfinancial Corporations During Trough-Peak-Trough and Peak-Trough-Peak Cycles, 1953-1981

	B/F (%)	B/I (%)	CMD/MVE (%)
TPT Cycles (five)			
1: (1954.4-1958.4)	29.0	27.3	36.2
2: (1958.4-1961.1)	29.2	28.1	33.4
3: (1961.1-1970.10)	38.6	34.6	33.4
4: (1970.10-1975.1)	55.2	48.9	50.7
5: (1975.1-1980.7)	45.7	42.0	74.3
PTP Cycles (six)			
1: (1953.7-1957.7)	26.0	23.9	37.9
2: (1957.7-1960.4)	29.7	28.8	39.9
3: (1960.4-1969.10)	36.9	32.9	32.5
4: (1969.10-1973.10)	50.3	46.1	41.5
5: (1973.10-1980.1)	49.6	44.5	73.3
6: (1980.1-1981.7)	43.3	41.5	71.1

B: Net Credit Borrowing
F: Fixed Investment
I: Capital Expenditures (Fixed Investment plus Inventory Investment)
CMD: Credit Market Debt Outstanding
MVE: Market Value of Corporate Equity

Source: C. J. Niggle (1989), Table 2, p. 217.

Empirical analyses show the close correlation between the behaviour of financial ratios and the performance of the economy during the cycle, which may be explained by an increase in the propensity to accumulate debt during expansions, following the reduction in the risk perceived by firms in periods of positive expectations on profits. The attitude of firms towards increasing indebtedness is encouraged by the banking system, in the early stage of an expansion. Unfortunately, it causes a progressive deterioration in financial structures, with increasing values of the debt-to-assets and debt-to-investment ratios and, in the late stage of an expansion, the shortening of the duration of debt, and a widespread state of illiquidity. In contractions, then, the opposite process takes place.

The information which has been collected by the various studies makes it possible to identify some of the persistent regularities which constitute the basic features of business cycles nowadays.

There is a fairly general consensus among scholars of different theoretical approaches about the so-called "stylized facts" of business cycles, which are summarised in the following list[5]:

a) there is a tendency towards a net growth of GNP in the long run. Growth takes place in the form of cyclical processes which are recurrent, although not constant in period;

b) the series of variables chosen as economic indicators may be classified as "coinciding", leading" or "lagging", according to their relative movement with respect to a reference series. Examples of the first category are the volume of output and the profits of firms working in different but related sectors, whilst variables that anticipate their movement with respect to a reference series can include the stock exchange rates, the value of shares sold on the New York Stock Exchange, or employment in hours per week in the manufacturing industries. Factory pay-rolls and medium-term money market rates are variables that move with at least a lag;

5 This list is analogous to the one in G. Gabish – H. Lorenz (1989). Some aspects are drawn from M. Dore in D. Glasner (1993).

c) business profits record greater amplitudes than other variables, as does the production of durable goods as compared with the production of non-durables;

d) the behaviour of agricultural production and the exploitation of natural resources and their respective prices appear to be deviating above average from the classification in coinciding, leading and lagging categories;

e) the aggregate price level and short-term interest rates, as well as buffer-stocks and capital investment, are pro-cyclical; monetary wages and prices move in the same direction and the former generally anticipate the latter; the unemployment rate is counter-cyclical; profits usually are pro-cyclical and in particular changes in profits per unit of sales anticipate changes in sales (in the same direction); long-term interest rates follow sluggishly in the same direction as the coinciding series; credit and monetary aggregates, as well as the income velocity of money, are pro-cyclical;

f) there is a high correlation and synchronisation of business cycles in many developed countries.

However, there are some other features which theorists seem unable to agree upon as to their actual relevance in characterising business cycles. The more important ones are the following:

g) labour productivity is pro-cyclical;

h) real wages move pro-cyclically – though, this is not unambiguous;

i) the ascending phase of the cycle is typically slower than the descending phase, so that observed cycles are asymmetric;

j) since World War II cycles have shown less amplitude.

The above "stylized facts" give a very precise picture of the fundamental economic relations that a model of business cycles should not violate in order to be as close as possible to reality and to be capable of providing a tool for understanding, and keeping under control, the mechanisms that govern the growth process of capitalist systems.

Of course, given the degree of complexity of the phenomenon in question and the consequent "size" of the analysis, it is rather problematic to allow for all the relationships into a single model. Instead, each model is quite distinct because of the emphasis it gives to those relationships which are considered crucial, rather than to others. These are not considered explicitly in the analysis, but are left to be dependent (all or in part) on the ones chosen.

CHAPTER II

Models and Methods in Endogenous Business Cycle Theory. An Overview of the Literature

2.1 – Preface

As mentioned in the Introduction, two different theoretical approaches dominate the current academic debate: the first, also known as the *Equilibrium Business Cycle* approach, is of neo-classical derivation, whereas the second moves within the Keynesian tradition, and has developed along different lines of research: the *New Keynesians* frameworks and the so-called *non-linear* or *endogenous* modelling[1].

The New Classics and the New Keynesians explain cyclical fluctuations mainly as the consequence of exogenous factors. Following the method introduced into economic analysis by E. Slutsky in 1927 and R. Frisch in 1933, both approaches distinguish the impulses from the propagation mechanisms, and focus on the source of the shocks (impulses) that set in motion the cyclical process. However the main differences between these two approaches may be summarised as follows.

The New Classics aim to account for the existence of cyclical fluctuations within the intertemporal Walrasian general equilibrium theoretical setting, following the seminal work by Lucas (1975) on *misperceptions*, the failure of

1 For a detailed survey and a comparative evaluation of the different approaches in the literature, see M. Dore (1993).

agents to distinguish changes in relative prices from changes in the aggregate price level. And yet, it is only with the *Real Business Cycle* models that one may talk in every respect of an *Equilibrium Business Cycle* theory. In fact, the models within this rather sophisticated analytical setting no longer have to rely on restricting assumptions on information, as in the Lucas model.

The so-called *Equilibrium Business Cycle* is explained by assuming the possibility of decomposing output into a trend component and a cyclical component, and expressing the former as the sum of exogenous shocks to productivity. Fluctuations, in any case, may occur only because of a given, yet arbitrary, lag structure of capital and of the technology shocks.

The New Keynesians' research project is in net contrast to the New Classics' theoretical view, and aims to give a theoretical microfoundation of the different behaviour of goods, labour and financial markets from the Walrasian theoretical paradigm. As is well known, within that theoretical setting perfect flexibility in the price system ensures that equilibrium in all markets is attained and an optimum allocation of resources, at the aggregate level, is fulfilled.

In the late Seventies, the New Keynesian approach started right from the critique of the sets of principles and methods in Lucas's theory, and focused on the behaviour of markets in the presence of imperfect competition and asymmetric information. This theoretical approach, originally directed towards issues in microeconomic analyses, was later successfully extended to the macro level, too, and nowadays is considered a very promising field of research and the most direct challenge to *Real Business Cycle* theory. As far as business cycle analysis is concerned, New Keynesians basically emphasize the role of exogenous impulses in generating cycles, in the presence of the aforementioned rigidities.

On the other hand, a different class of models in business cycle theory, the so-called *endogenous cycle* modelling, distinguishes itself for the emphasis given to the existence of mechanisms which are *endogenous* to the structure and to the performance of the economic systems. The aforesaid inner mechanisms are able to start up cyclical fluctuations which, at times, may lead to instability and "systemic" crises. This field of the research goes back to some pre-Keynesian analyses which, in earlier times, aimed to highlight endogenous determinants of business fluctuations. In the Forties, some authors started directing their research towards non-linear analytical frameworks, following the seminal contributions by Kalecki, Hicks, Kaldor and Goodwin[2]. Indeed, the Kalecki and Hicks models have a typically linear structure, but introduce boundaries to the motion of the system, the "floor" and the "ceiling", that make the overall system non-linear. As stressed by several authors, the non-linearity stems from factors that are not derived from the model itself. Besides, that class of models needs to rely on the continuous presence of exogenous disturbances in order to exhibit permanent fluctuations.

Non-linear modelling appears to be more suitable for the purpose of representing the actual behaviour of the economy over a cycle, which is characterised by permanent, although not constant, fluctuations rather than by explosive or damped fluctuations, which are the typical features of linear models.

This point explains the renewed interest in non-linear dynamics in more recent years, thanks to the developments in the application of mathematical methods and concepts to economic analysis, in particular with reference to the study of dynamic systems. Building on the aforementioned seminal theoretical contributions to the analysis of endogenous cycles, several models have been elaborated in the subsequent developments in this field of research. These recent

2 M. Kalecki (1937), (1939), (1943); N. Kaldor (1940); J. Hicks (1950); R. Goodwin (1948), (1951), (1967).

models take into account prices, financial markets, technology and so on, and are generally characterised by increasing analytical complexity. Very often, then, the "size" of the models have made numerical simulations necessary, given the difficulty or impossibility of deriving formal solutions to the analysis. Hence, the earlier contributions in the literature remain a constant reference in the study of business cycles, since they provide a "minimal" analytical framework for the emergence of a persistent oscillatory behaviour.

The present Chapter surveys these models in the literature[3], in order to highlight some of the relevant factors in business cycles which in the course of the following Chapters will be analysed and developed further.

The more recent literature on non-linear dynamics has developed along several lines of research. In particular[4], it is possible to distinguish a class of models in which fluctuations are governed by a (non-linear) multiplier-accelerator mechanism, as in Goodwin (1948, 1951), and Hicks (1950). In a second group of models wage-shares dynamics and employment dynamics are linked together, as in the Goodwin "predatory-prey" model (1967). Some authors have developed the original Kaldor scheme (1940), based on the non-linear income-investment interaction, whereas others have used models of the Kalecki type (1971), where the profit-investment relation is crucial. A further alternative explored in non-linear dynamics is within the context of the overlapping generations modelling, as in Benhabib-Day (1982) and Grandmont (1985).

In what follows, the Kalecki (1971) and Hicks (1950) models are reviewed first, because of their importance in the subsequent developments of the literature. As mentioned above, these models rely on the existence of continuous

---

3 On this point, see A. Medio (1979); G. Gabish – H. Lorenz (1989); S. Sordi (1990); M. Dore (1993).

4 See W. Semmler (1989), Introduction.

shocks to start the cycle and to keep it up permanently. The Goodwin (1951), Kaldor (1940) and Goodwin (1967) models are the next to be presented, and in these cycles are generated endogenously.

The last part concentrates on models of business cycles in which money and financial markets are considered. First of all, the Di Matteo (1984) and Asada (1989) models, which extend the basic Goodwin (1967) framework by introducing money and prices. Finally, the literature stressing the issues of indebtedness, financial fragility and instability in the cyclical process will be introduced, with particular reference to the Franke-Semmler (1989) model.

2.2 – The Role of Real Factors in the Analysis of Economic Fluctuations

The business cycle in Kalecki

Kalecki worked several models of business cycles. The first model, which dates back to 1935, has a linear structure[5]. It was later reformulated in the non-linear versions of the 1937 and 1939 models, which fundamentally share its basic idea. The *Studies in Economic Dynamics* of 1943 represents an important stage in the evolution of Kalecki's scientific thought, as he worked on the theory of distribution and investment with a view to explaining cyclical and long run changes jointly. This effort culminated in the *Theory of Economic Dynamics* (1954).

Linear models have a basic structure which is formally very similar to the multiplier-accelerator schemes, and therefore show the typical dynamic

5 The theory was developed in *Proba Teorji Konjunctury*, a monograph published in 1933 in Warsaw and later presented in "Essai d'une théorie du mouvement cyclique des affaires" [*Revue d'Economie Politique*, 1935, (pp. 285-305)], and formalised in the paper "A Macrodynamic Theory of Business Cycle" [*Econometrica*, 1935, (pp. 327-44)].

behaviour of this class of models, that is, damped or explosive fluctuations, depending on the values of the relevant parameters. In fact, in order to exhibit permanent fluctuations they have to rely on continuous exogenous shock.

A common feature in Kalecki is the subdivision of the analysis into two logical periods: in the first place, the determination of a single period equilibrium and, secondly, the connection of all the periods in dynamic sequence. The short run is a "Keynesian" equilibrium, in the sense that at the corresponding level of income savings equal investment. However, this equilibrium is not relevant *per se*, but rather as a link in the long-run sequence in which investment acts as the connecting mechanism.

In the early 1935 model, Kalecki assumed the existence of a fixed time lag, θ, between the decision to invest and the installation of new equipment[6]. In this case, the change in the capital stock at time $t+\theta$ is equal to the investment decision at time t, $I^D(t)$:

$$\dot{K}(t+\theta) = I^D(t) \quad \text{or} \quad \dot{K}(t) = I^D(t-\theta).$$

Investment is assumed to be a function of income and of the capital stock, according to the following linear relation:

$$I^D(t) = asY(t) - kK(t) + \varepsilon$$

6 This assumption about technology, drawn from A. Aftalion (*Les crises périodiques de surproduction*, Paris: Marcel Rivière, 1913) is the way Kalecki introduces dynamics into the model, since it leads to a second-order difference equation. In Aftalion the lags between orders and the production of investment goods determine the *over-capitalisation* and *under-capitalisation* crises during the cycle. Kalecki, however, prefers to consider the role of effective demand in the cycle. This role is neglected in Aftalion, where the productive capacity is assumed to be always at the full utilisation level and adjustments take place only through price fluctuations.

where s is the marginal propensity to save, a and k are constant coefficients and ε is a trend component. The above relations, together with the condition of equilibrium between the value of production of the investment goods and savings, yield the mixed difference-differential equation:

$$\dot{K}(t) = a/\theta K(t) - (k + a/\theta)K(t-\theta)\ a/\theta$$

and, by setting $\theta = 1$, it becomes:

$$\dot{K}(t) = aK(t) - (k + a)K(t-1).$$

In order for the model to generate harmonic oscillations the complex roots of the characteristic equation must have zero real part, which would occur only for exactly one numerical value of coefficient k. For any other value of the latter, the behaviour of the system is characterised by damped or explosive oscillations. The case of explosive oscillations is in fact excluded, since they do not seem to be realistic in the actual behaviour of capitalist economies, so the model exhibits damped fluctuations, in the case of complex roots, and therefore it has to rely on external shocks in order to exhibit persistent fluctuations[7].

The 1954 model[8] also has the same kind of drawbacks. The kind of cyclical fluctuations implied by the investment function depends on the value of the

7 Cf. R. G. Allen (1963) for details on the analytical solution of the model. And see also T. Asada (1994) for a reformulation of it with monetary factors within the context of a system of mixed difference-differential equations, where the stability results are re-examined in light of more recent advances in mathematical methods.

8 Cf. Chapters 11, 13, 14, 15. Here the variables of the investment function are the following: the level of current savings, linked to profits (with one period lag), rather than to income; the rate of change of profits and the increase in the capital stock. Whereas the first variable is a "reinvestment factor", the second is similar to the accelerator principle, although different in its economic foundation. In fact the latter is

parameters involved and on the time lags of the equation. Yet, in any case permanent fluctuations may last only in the presence of the effect of erratic disturbances that contrast the dampening tendency which is inherent in the fundamental mechanism[9].

In order to overcome the typical shortcoming of models with constant coefficients, that is, being unable to exhibit permanent fluctuations, Kalecki proposed some non-linear versions of the earlier 1935 model. Basically, the author introduced an *S*-shaped investment function of the type described in Figure (2.1). The curve representing the investment decisions at time *t*, $I^D(t)$, is parametrically influenced by variations in the stock of capital $K(t)$: the level of investment decisions (on the ordinates) is lower at corresponding higher levels of $K(t)$, for each level of output (on the abscissae).

The graph shows the set of the short-run equilibrium points, $Y(t) = f(I(t))$, for the case of a linear function, with $\theta = 1$. As in the 1935 model, $f(I(t)) = f(I^D(t-1))$. The intersection of the two curves yields the long-run equilibrium level Y^*. A deviation from the equilibrium point starts up an adjustment process towards Y^* if this is stable, and if the level of the stock of capital is kept constant[10]. The setting in motion of a cyclical process is due to the fact that at Y^l the level of investment is below depreciation, and this brings about a decrease in the stock of capital. The process is reversed when the level of investment exceeds the amount of depreciation - that is, the long-run

generally identified with the need for firms to adapt their productive capacity to changes in demand, whereas in Kalecki's opinion firms usually operate below the full utilisation of plants, so that the foundation of the accelerator principle should instead be sought in the improvement of profit expectations and in the consequent gains to be obtained by overcoming the drawbacks of imperfect competition.

9 M. Kalecki (1954), Ch. 11.

10 Cf. G. Gabish – W. Lorenz (1989), pp. 74-75 for analytical details.

equilibrium level - and capital increases over time so that the $I^D(t)$ curve shifts down.

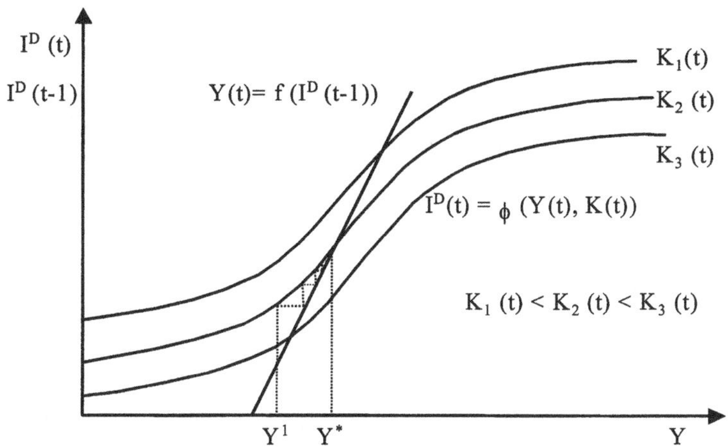

Figure (2.1). *The non-linear Kalecki model*

One shortcoming of this non-linear version is that, since the long-run equilibrium is stable, the system converges to it monotonically after an exogenous shock, unless specific assumptions are made about the value of the relevant parameters. For instance, in the case presented above, a sufficiently strong shift of the I^D curve is required in order for the cyclical process to be initiated.

The non-linear Hicks model

In 1950 Hicks restated the multiplier-accelerator principle introduced by Samuelson (1939) adding some variants, but basically leaving the structure of the model unchanged. It is still made up of one equation for consumption, with income entering with a one period lag, one equation for induced investment, which is now a function of the change in total demand in the last two periods, and one equation that states the equilibrium condition between savings and investment. The model may be specified in the form of a second-order difference equation, and as usual the dynamic behaviour will depend on the parameter regime.

Like any other linear model with constant (structural) parameters over time, the shortcomings of this model are that it exhibits oscillations only in the case of complex roots and that oscillations are permanent only for the exact values of the parameters involved[11].

In order to overcome these drawbacks, and excluding the case of damped fluctuations, Hicks assumed the existence of boundaries to the motion of the investment function employed in the linear model, which prevent the system from becoming explosive.

The introduction of these boundaries, called the "ceiling" and the "floor", is necessary to limit the range of admissible values of the investment function over the cycle. In this way, during expansions and upper parts of contractions the acceleration mechanism is at work, whereas during downswings net investment is determined on the basis that the decrease in investment cannot exceed the fixed limit of depreciation.

Hicks assumed the existence of an autonomous component of investment I^a, which grows at a constant rate r; the equilibrium path of income Y^* is defined on the basis of that rate r. As to the "ceiling", it corresponds to the growth path of income consistent with the full employment of resources, whereas the "floor"

11 In P. Samuelson (1939) by solving the characteristic equation a *critical condition* is obtained which depends on two parameters, the marginal propensity to consume and the accelerator coefficient, whereas in Hicks it involves only the accelerator coefficient.

is the path along which net investment is given by the autonomous component alone.

Therefore, two investment functions are defined, the first valid for the upswing of the cycle, the second for the downswing:

$$I^n = \beta(Y_{t-1} - Y_{t-2}) + I^a \qquad [2.1]$$

$$I^n = \max[\beta(Y_{t-1} - Y_{t-2}) + I^a,\ I^a - D];\ \ D = \text{constant} \qquad [2.2]$$

where D stands for the constant, and exogenously given, amount of depreciation. As equation [2.2] shows, in the initial stage of a contraction the accelerator is at work, according to the value of the coefficient β; eventually, when the decrease in investment, following the fall in income, exceeds the level of depreciation, net investment is given by autonomous investment and the amount of depreciation.

The behaviour of the system is illustrated in Figure (2.2), starting from a generic initial point P_o. Here, income is growing because of the constant growth in the autonomous component of investment I^a, and this determines a rise in induced investment via the accelerator, on the basis of equation [2.1], and consequently, an increase in the growth rate of income which exceeds the rate at which autonomous investment is growing. As soon as the full utilisation of resources is reached, the trajectory of the system approaches the boundary of the "ceiling", the $\overline{Y}$ - path in the graph. Since the growth rate of income is constant at that point, induced investment is zero and consequently the growth rate of investment decreases, as does the associated growth rate of income. The downturn is amplified by the working of the accelerator, until the fall in investment leads to a decrease in income up to the point that net investment will be determined by equation [2.2], and the trajectory of the system will move below the equilibrium growth path Y^*, towards the "floor" $\underline{Y}$. The latter is the income path determined by autonomous investment and depreciation only, that is with zero induced investment. As time elapses, since income keeps growing at positive growth rates while moving along this path, the conditions for positive induced investment are restored, and a new cycle is set in motion.

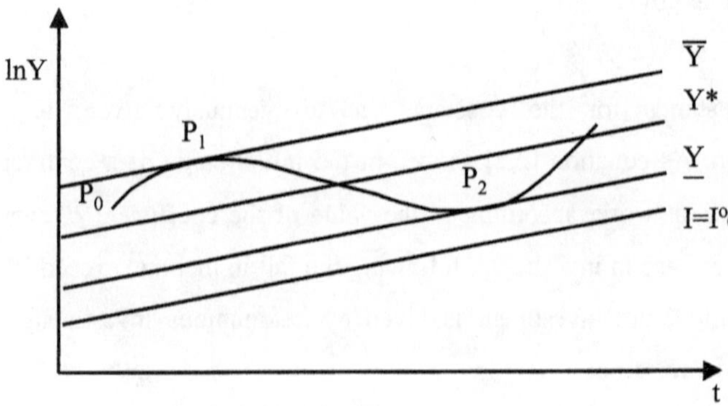

Figure 2.2. *Hicks's non-linear accelerator*

Although this model is capable of generating fluctuations independently of the specific values of the involved parameters, it has a few drawbacks which have been highlighted by different scholars. First of all, the persistence of the cycle relies on the assumption that autonomous investment will continue to grow over time. In fact, were it constant during the cycle, then the system would not be able to recover from the "floor". Moreover, the boundary given by the "ceiling" is not derived from the model itself, so that different rates of growth give rise to fluctuations of varying amplitude[12].

12 On this point, cf. the comment in G. Gabish – H. Lorenz (1989). For a detailed discussion of this type of non-linearities, see W. Baumol (1958).

The non-linear acceleration and the cyclical process in Goodwin

In an article published in *Econometrica* in 1951, Goodwin presented a series of business cycle models, starting from a very simplified basic version in which the non-linear acceleration principle is illustrated, and then developing some variants of the basic model.

Despite the relative simplicity of the basic model illustrated in the present section, it clearly contains the typical features of non-linear oscillators, which may be summarised as follows[13]. First of all, the equilibrium position is unstable and a "limit-cycle" exists to which all trajectories converge, so that the system never explodes nor dampens, but oscillates within given boundaries, because of the non-linearity. The oscillations, started by minimal disturbances, are persistent, that is, they do not need to be sustained continuously by external factors. Moreover, the emergence of cycles does not rely on the "initial conditions" of the problem, nor on the introduction of a specific lag-structure in the analytical specification of the model.

The cyclical mechanism is such that the boom creates the conditions which lead to its own dissolving, and the recession creates the circumstances for the recovery. This is due to the nature of investment decisions: when investment is too high capitalists desire more capital, whereas when it is too low they wish to get rid of their capital.

Following Goodwin, the model is here illustrated.

There is one equation for desired capital K^*, which is assumed to be proportional to income Y; one equation for consumption C, linear in income; one equation for income, equal to the sum of consumption and net investment. The latter equals the change in the capital stock, that is $dK/dt = \dot{K}$. Formally:

13 In the Appendixes A.1 and A.2 of the present work the basic characteristics of non-linear oscillators are discussed in more detail.

$$K^* = \kappa Y$$

$$C = \alpha + \beta Y \qquad [2.3]$$

$$Y = C + \dot{K}$$

where α, β, and κ are positive constants. The function describing the behaviour of net investment I^n is piece-wisely defined, which makes the model quasi-non-linear. Depending on the difference between actual and desired capital over the cycle, an adjustment process takes place leading to different values for net investment I^n over time. In particular, the above values range from the capacity of the investment goods industry less the fixed amount of depreciation $\bar{I} - D$ when actual capital is smaller then the desired capital, to the value zero when the two quantities coincide, and finally to a negative value equal to depreciation when the actual stock of capital exceeds the desired stock and gross investment is zero. Thus, the resulting net investment function is:

$$I^n = \begin{cases} \bar{I} - D\,, & K < K^* \\ 0, & K = K^* \\ -D, & K > K^*. \end{cases} \qquad [2.4]$$

Consequently, the desired capital stock K^*, being a function of actual income, assumes the following different values over the cycle:

$$K^* = \begin{cases} \dfrac{\kappa\alpha}{1-\beta} + \dfrac{\kappa}{1-\beta}(\bar{I} - D), & K < K^* \\ \dfrac{\kappa\alpha}{1-\beta}, & K = K^* \\ \dfrac{\kappa\alpha}{1-\beta} + \dfrac{\kappa}{1-\beta}(-D), & K > K^*. \end{cases} \qquad [2.5]$$

The system exhibits a cyclical motion which is characterised by a discontinuity at the "ceiling" and at the "floor". This is illustrated by Goodwin through the graph shown in Figure (2.3).

Point E is an unstable equilibrium, with $K = K^*$. Were a small disturbance $\Delta K > 0$ to occur which made $K > K^*$, then the decrease in net investment would equal the amount of depreciation, that is, it would be $I^n = -D$.

The associated level of the desired capital stock would be given, accordingly, by the third equation of system [2.5], that is: $\frac{\kappa\alpha}{1-\beta} + \frac{\kappa}{1-\beta}(-D) < \frac{\kappa\alpha}{1-\beta}$, corresponding to point A in the graph.

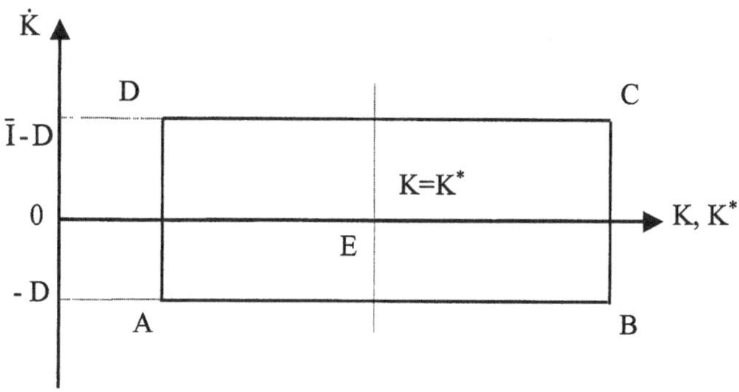

Figure 2.3. *The quasi-non-linear business cycle in Goodwin*

The decrease in investment would then proceed until the actual stock of capital equals the new value of the desired stock at point A. Hence, as soon as the latter point is reached, the desired capital stock would jump initially to the value $\frac{\kappa\alpha}{1-\beta}$. Eventually, since the actual stock at point A is below the new level K^*, the latter would increase up to the new level $\frac{\kappa\alpha}{1-\beta} + \frac{\kappa}{1-\beta}(\bar{I} - D)$, as in the first equation in system [2.5]. Hence, net investment jumps from point A to point D and remains at the "ceiling" level, until the actual capital stock reaches point C. Since, at this point, the equality between actual and desired stocks is once again restored, the latter changes to the lower level and again the system returns to the situation with $K > K^*$, implying the new level $K^* = \frac{\kappa\alpha}{1-\beta} + \frac{\kappa}{1-\beta}(\bar{I} - D)$, corresponding to point B. The decrease in investment continues, until point A is reached again.

The behaviour of the stock of capital, output and net investment is illustrated in Figure (2.4).

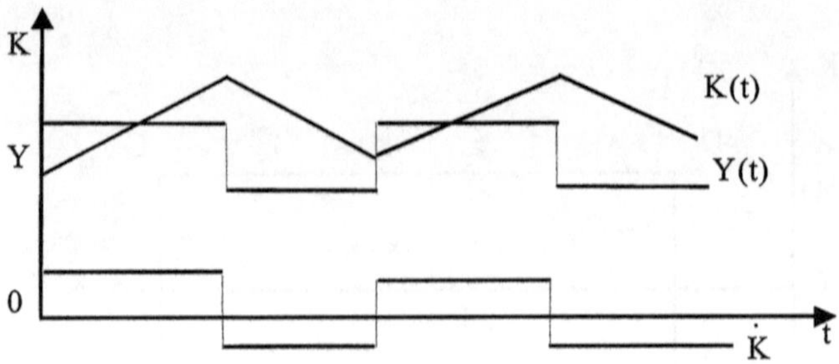

Figure 2.4. *The behaviour of the stock of capital, output and net investment in Goodwin (1951).*

Since the model is capable of generating persistent self-sustaining oscillations even in its simplest form, it has encouraged modifications and extensions in different directions. For instance, one could remove the discontinuities in the investment function[14]. A very simple way of doing this is to specify the investment function with the arctangent, a function that has the

14 Cf. G. Rodano (1986).

desired analytical features. So, in discrete terms, the model would assume the following form:

$$Y(t) = C(t) + I(t),$$

$$C(t) = \alpha + \beta Y(t),$$

$$I(t) = K(t) - K(t - 1),$$

$$I(t) = \eta \, arctg \, [K^*(t) - K(t - 1)],$$

$$K^*(t) = \gamma Y(t - 1).$$

The system may be put in the reduced form:

$$Y(t) = \alpha /(1 - \beta) + \eta /(1 - \beta) \, arctg \, [\gamma Y(t - 1) - K(t - 1)],$$

$$K(t) = K(t - 1) + \eta \, arctg[\gamma Y (t - 1) - K(t - 1)]. \qquad [2.6]$$

Simple algebraic calculations lead to the steady-state values for output $Y^* = \alpha /(1-\beta)$ and the stock of capital $K^* = \gamma Y^*$. The phase diagram of the model is illustrated in Figure (2.5), showing the two curves $\Delta Y(t) = 0$ and $\Delta K(t) = 0$, along which output and the stock of capital, respectively, are constant.

The intersection of the two curves gives the steady-state position of the system, which is unstable. In fact, at points to the left of the $\Delta Y(t) = 0$ curve, output is increasing, for a given $K(t)$, due to the effective demand principle, whereas to the right it is falling. On the other hand, at all points above the $\Delta K(t) = 0$ curve, capital is decreasing, for a given $Y(t)$, because it exceeds the desired level, whereas below the curve it is increasing. Yet, the motion of the system is bounded, that is, a limit-cycle exists to which all trajectories converge[15].

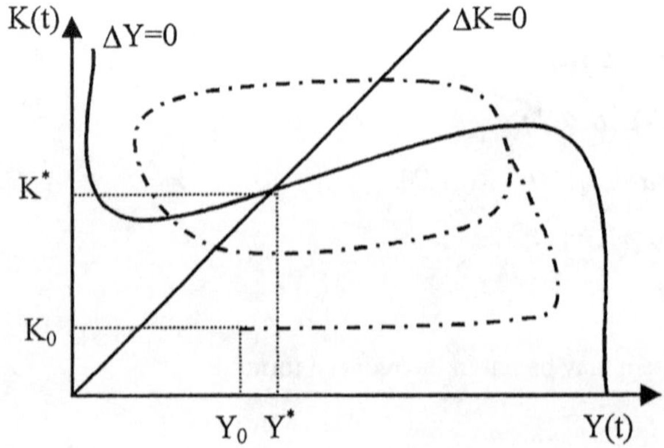

Figure 2.5. *The phase-diagram for the Goodwin (1951) model*

One of the many possible extensions of the model which have already been explored is the work by Thio (1984), in which the basic Goodwin (1951) model is modified in order to allow for cyclical growth through the consideration of technical progress. For this purpose, the author assumes that the investment function fluctuates within "moving" boundaries, in order to take into account the changes in the capacity of the investment goods industry. This enables a better representation of a growing economy. Moreover, the "development factors" of the model are identified in the technology changes which modify the structure of capital, making the technique more or less capital intensive in the different cases with the various associated assumptions on labour saving. The author shows that the ability of the model to generate growth is linked to the condition that

15 See the Appendix (A.3) for the proof of the existence of a "limit-cycle".

changes in technology and productivity generate additional demand, in particular via the labour market. In fact, it may happen that the aforesaid changes give rise to structural unemployment, thus acting negatively on the growth rate of the economy, in the absence of policy interventions aimed to sustain the level of aggregate demand.

The business cycle in Kaldor

In the models discussed above the domain of the investment function is not the same over the full range of the cycle, and the systems are piece-wise linear or quasi-non-linear. The Kaldor model (1940) is among the first "pure" non-linear models of business cycle.

Kaldor assumed that both investment and savings are non-linear functions of the level of economic activity. The S-shape of the two functions is explained in the following way. As far as investment is concerned, the effect of a change in the level of economic activity is small at both low and high levels of economic activity. This is due to the existence of unutilised productive capacity in the first case, and because of the emergence of diseconomies of various types, in the second case. Similarly, savings are supposed to be highly sensitive to changes in the level of economic activity when the latter is low as well as when it is high. In the first case, this is associated with the need to maintain a certain level of consumption and, in the second case, with a shift in income distribution in favour of profits, which leads to an above-average level of aggregate savings. The dynamics of the Kaldor model may be illustrated by means of Figure (2.6).

Here the S-shaped investment and savings curves are plotted as non-linear functions of the level of real income[16] X, and their position in the plane is

16 Kaldor assumed that the "economic activity" is correlated somehow to real income. So this expression will be used throughout the presentation of the model.

parametrically influenced by the changing level of the stock of capital *K*. The investment function *I*(*X*) shifts downwards at higher levels of the capital stock, for a given level of real income, because the associated fall in the marginal efficiency of capital determines a decrease in investment at each level of income. On the contrary, the saving function *S*(*X*) shifts upwards, but the author does not provide a convincing argument to support this assumption.

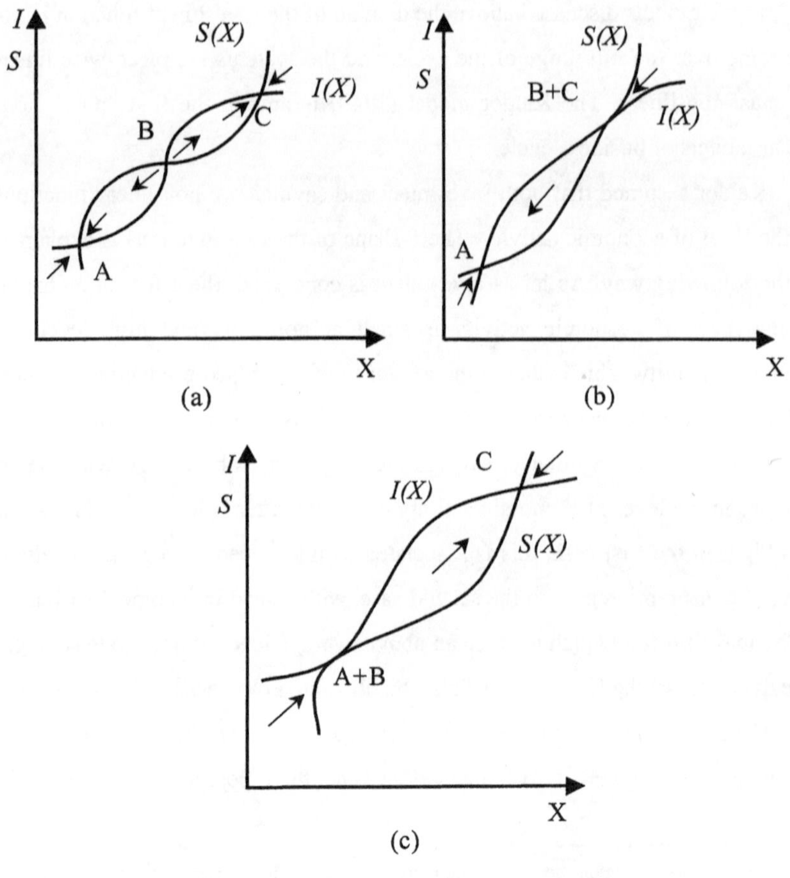

Figure 2.6. *The cycle in the Kaldor model*

At the intersection of the two curves there are three equilibrium points in the system. Of these, points A and C are locally asymptotically stable, whereas B is an unstable equilibrium, as the arrows of Figure (2.6a) show. The cyclical motion is governed by the adjustment process in the goods market which drives the system through subsequent equilibrium points, as is illustrated in Figure (2.6). The equilibria are determined at each new $I(X)$-$S(X)$ intersection, following the shift of the two curves over the cycle, as described above.

Let us assume that the system is initially at point C (figure (a)), where with a high level of income, investment and the capital stock are high, too. Therefore, the $I(X)$ function shifts downwards and the $S(X)$ function upwards (figure (b)) so that point C moves gradually downwards until the two curves become tangent and points B and C coincide (figure (b)). As is evident, on both sides of this point savings are greater than investment, that is, an excess supply in the goods market exists, which makes this point unstable. Therefore, a minimal accidental negative shock drives the system towards point A, where the fall in the level of income comes to an end. Here, because the capital stock has decreased to the point that profitable conditions for investment are restored, the $I(X)$ moves upwards until points A and B coincide (figure (c)). During the recovery, the increase in the level of savings moves the $S(X)$ function upwards, and a new cycle is started up again[17].

17 In Chang-Smith (1971) the Kaldor model is reformulated as a Liénard-van der Pol type equation, in order to prove the existence of at least one limit-cycle. The fundamental relations of the model are formalised in the following way:

$$I = I(y, k); \quad S = S(y, k) \qquad I_y > 0,\ I_k < 0,\ S_y > 0,\ S_k > 0 \qquad [2.7]$$

$$\mu \dot{y} = I(y,k) - S(y,k) \qquad [2.8]$$

$$\dot{k} = \bar{I}(y,k). \qquad [2.9]$$

In equation [2.7] investment and ex-ante savings are functions of income y and of the capital stock k; in equation [2.8] the disequilibrium between investment and savings is corrected by changes in the level of income; in equation [2.9] the change in the stock of capital equals the realised investment $\bar{I}$. Moreover, the following are assumed to hold: $I_y > S_y$, $I_K > S_K$. For analytical details, cf. the Appendix (A.4).

The criticism generally made of the Kaldor model concerns the assumption that the sensitivity of investment to income is higher then the sensitivity of savings to income at the equilibrium point, which is given in the condition $I_y > S_y$. This hypothesis, which is required to make the equilibrium unstable, is necessary for a limit-cycle to exist. Yet, it is not sufficiently motivated by the author, and hence it may appear arbitrary.

The Goodwin growth cycle model

In his 1967 contribution Goodwin elaborated a model in which the mechanism of business cycles is governed by the conflict between workers and capitalists over income distribution. As a starting point, Goodwin used the studies by Lotka (1925) and Volterra (1931) on the behavioural dynamics of two species of fish, one the *prey* and the other the *predator* in the biological chain, whose interdependence may be represented using a system of differential equations of the following type:

$$\dot{x} = ax - bxy$$
$$\dot{y} = -cy + dxy$$

with *a, b, c,* and *d* as positive constants. The first equation describes the behaviour of the *prey* population, indicated as x, the second of the *predator* population, denoted as y. The specification of the equations is such that were the predator population y to become extinct, the prey x would grow exponentially at rate a (the first equation). On the other hand, were the prey x to die out, then the predator population y would decrease exponentially at rate c (the second equation).

The system described by the Lotka-Volterra equations has the characteristic that each trajectory is a closed orbit, except the equilibrium point (x^*, y^*), and the origin of the axes. Moreover, the equilibrium point is stable. In Figure (2.7) the closed orbits of the system for different initial population conditions (that is, at $t = 0$) are illustrated.

By borrowing the concept of the predator-prey relationship from the biological sciences, Goodwin interpreted the cyclical behaviour of the economy as the resultant of the conflict over income distribution which originates in the clash of interests between the working class and the capitalists, within the theoretical perspective of the "Classics", starting from Smith up to Ricardo and Marx.

In the model Goodwin makes the distinction between the workers, on the one side, who spend all their income, in the form of wages, on consumption, and the capitalists, on the other side, who receive and save entirely the profits from firms, that is the value of the production once total wages have been paid.

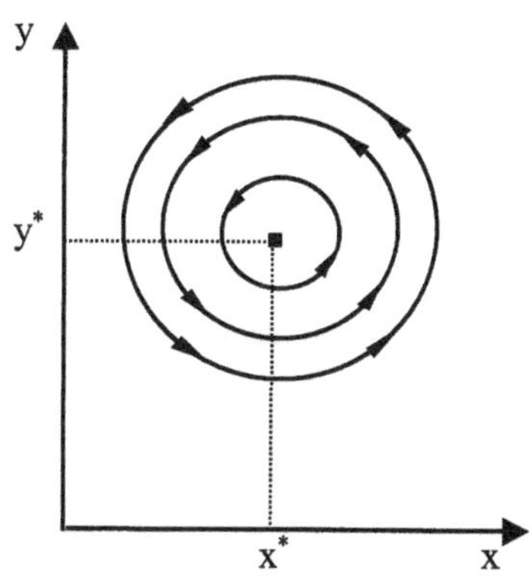

Figure 2.7. *Closed orbits in the Goodwin model (1967)*

The price of goods is normalised and equal to unity. Define as wL/Y the share of wages on total output, with w as the money wage, L employment and Y

total output, and assume that labour productivity a grows at a constant rate ϕ, and that labour supply N grows at rate n; then, the equilibrium condition between savings and investment is stated in the following form:

$$\dot{K} = S = (1 - wL/Y)Y = (1 - w/a)Y,$$

where $\dot{K}$ indicates the change in the stock of capital - that is, net investment - and the expression in brackets indicates the profit-share of total output, the wage-share being, by definition, the wage-productivity ratio.

By setting σ as the capital-output ratio K/Y, the rate of growth of the capital stock is given by:

$$\dot{K}/K = (1 - w/a)Y/K = (1 - w/a)/\sigma.$$

With a constant value of σ, the above expression is equal to the growth rate of output, that is: $\dot{K}/K = \dot{Y}/Y$.

Having denoted the wage-share as $u \equiv w/a$, and the employment rate as $v \equiv L/N$, Goodwin is able to describe the dynamics of the system through a system of two differential equations in the variables u and v, the structure of which is similar to the Lotka-Volterra equations.

Given the assumptions of the model, the following relations are obtained[18]:

$$\dot{v}/v = \dot{L}/L - \dot{N}/N = \frac{1-u}{\sigma} - (\phi + n) \qquad [2.14]$$

$$\dot{u}/u = \dot{w}/w - \dot{a}/a = \dot{w}/w - \phi. \qquad [2.15]$$

---

18 Since $\dot{K}/K = \dot{Y}/Y$ and, by definition, $L = Y/a$, in the first equation the following holds: $\dot{L}/L = \dot{Y}/Y - \phi$.

Goodwin assumes that the conflict over income distribution may be formally specified in terms of a Phillips curve, relating the growth rate of money wages to the employment rate, that is:

$$\dot{w}/w = f(v), \lim f(v)_{v \to 1} = \infty, \lim f(v)_{v \to 0} = w < 0, \frac{\delta f}{\delta v} > 0. \qquad [2.16]$$

By considering a linear approximation of equation [2.16], equations [2.14] and [2.15] may be reformulated as:

$$\begin{aligned} \dot{v} &= [1/\sigma - (\phi + n) - u/\sigma]v \\ \dot{u} &= [-(\phi + \gamma) + \rho v]u. \end{aligned} \qquad [2.17]$$

This system gives the two Lotka-Volterra equations in which v is the prey and u is the predator. The economic interpretation of these two equations is immediate. As v tends to zero the growth rate of the wage-share u tends to zero too. This, of course, encourages employment, given the low level of labour costs.

It is possible to illustrate graphically the behaviour of the system.

To simplify the notation denote $s \equiv 1/\sigma - (\phi + n)$, $b \equiv 1/\sigma$ and $c \equiv \gamma + a$, so that the equations in system [2.17] become:

$$\begin{aligned} \dot{v} &= (s - bu)v \\ \dot{u} &= -(c - \rho v)u. \end{aligned}$$

It is possible to eliminate time by considering the ratio of the two equations above. Some algebra leads to:

$$\frac{-u(c - \rho v)dv}{v} = \frac{(s - bu)du}{u},$$

and by integrating both sides the following expressions are given:

$$-c\log v + \rho v + \log A = s\log u - bu,$$

$$v^{-c}e^{\rho v}A = u^{s}e^{-bu} \qquad [2.17a]$$

where $A = v_0^c u_0^s e^{-\rho v_0 - b u_0}$ is the constant of integration.

The method illustrated by Volterra for the graphical analysis of the system consists in redefining both sides of equation [2.17a] with the new variables h and z. The corresponding graphs are illustrated in Figure (2.8) by the curves C_1 and C_2, respectively. There are four quadrants. In the first the relation between u and v is plotted; in the second z is plotted as a function of u and in the fourth h as a function of v. The third quadrant serves as a link between the second and the fourth, via the 45° line, since in equation [2.17a] $z = h$. Therefore, the maximum point on the C_1 curve at D maps onto the two points D' and D'' on the C_2 curve, which constitute the bounds of v, and which give points P and P' on the C_3 curve of the first quadrant. Similarly, to the minimum point on the C_2 curve at B, there correspond the two points B' and B'' on the C_1 curve, via the 45° line, which yield points Q and Q' on the C_3 curve of the first quadrant. The latter define the bounds within which u may vary. For different initial values of u and v there is a whole family of closed orbits around point T, which constitutes the solution associated to the equality between the minimum of h and the maximum of z.

The motion along the C_3 curve is anti-clockwise. In fact, setting $v \equiv c/\rho$, the second equation of system [2.17] becomes:

$$\frac{\dot{u}}{u} = -\left[c - m\left(\frac{c}{\rho}\right)\right] = 0, \quad \text{which implies:}$$

$$\frac{\dot{u}}{u} < 0 \ \text{ for } v < \frac{c}{\rho}; \quad \frac{\dot{u}}{u} > 0 \ \text{ for } v > \frac{c}{\rho}.$$

Therefore, the wage-share is decreasing along the trajectory to the left of the *Q-Q'* line, whereas it is increasing to the right of the line. As the employment rate *v* increases, the wage-share *u* decreases from point *P* to point *Q* and, eventually, increases reaching point *P'*, where *v* is at a maximum.

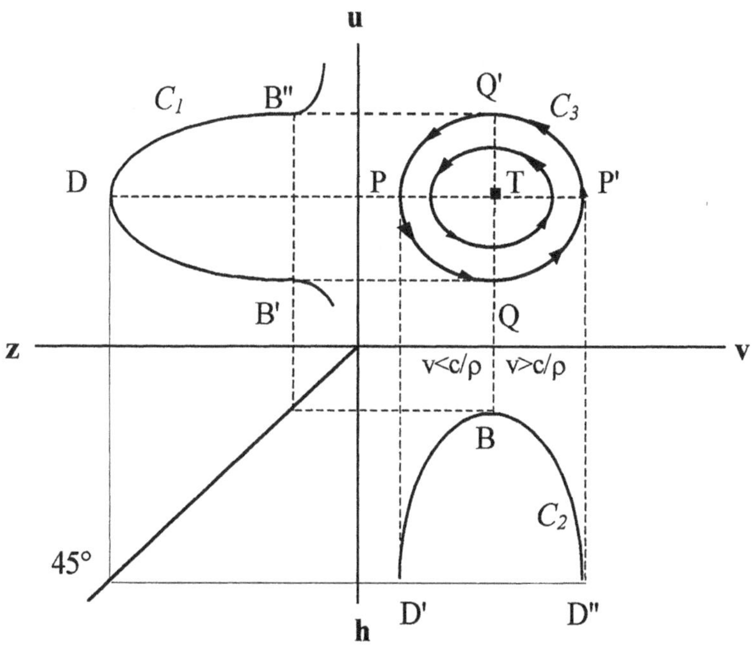

Figure 2.8. *The growth cycle in Goodwin*

The cyclical process takes place along the trajectories sketched in the diagram: the early expansive phase is identified by the *P-Q* arch, where the employment rate is growing following the expansion of production and profits. At Q the wage-share is at a minimum and, consequently, the profit-share reaches its maximum level.

As employment increases, the bargaining power of the labour-force predominates, thus causing a shift in income distribution in its own favour. The profit-share, therefore, decreases until point P' is reached, where the employment rate is at its maximum level.

From that point on the system moves along the trajectory towards point Q', where profits are at a minimum while the employment rate starts decreasing steadily. The contraction goes on until point P is reached once again, and the conditions for a recovery led by the growth of profits are restored.

From one cycle to the other the growth rate of output is positive, implying that expansions are stronger than contractions. In the long run, employment grows at the growth rate of the labour supply, and real wages increase since the wage-share of income is constant and the growth rate of output is positive.

This model has drawn a large consensus among scholars and students of business cycles, who have much appreciated its ability to deal with such a complex issue within a relatively simple analytical framework. For this reason it has been widely studied and extended to more sophisticated versions in the subsequent developments of business cycle models. It is worth noting, among others, the work by Desai (1973), in which prices and the possibility of a variable capital-output ratio are introduced, the contribution by Vellupilai (1979) on the stability properties of the Goodwin model and the effects of a non-linear Phillips curve, and the analysis of Flaschel (1984) on the role of variable goods prices and money illusion into a Goodwin-type model.[19]

---

19 Some very interesting contributions, in addition to the ones mentioned in the text, are in the volume edited by R. M. Goodwin – M. Krüger – A. Vercelli (1984).

2.3 – The Introduction of Money in Business Cycle Modelling

Some extensions of the Goodwin model. The contribution by Di Matteo

A study of the effects of the introduction of money and prices into the Goodwin model was made first by Di Matteo (1984) and later by Asada (1989). In this section the analysis developed by Di Matteo will be described briefly.

The author suggests an investment function in which money is included and modifies the model by adding one equation for the growth rate of prices and the equations for the monetary sector, as in the following system:

$$
\begin{aligned}
& I = y - (\frac{w}{p})L + \psi k(\theta - \mu\frac{\dot{y}}{y}) \\
& \frac{\dot{p}}{p} = \frac{\beta}{1+\beta}(\frac{\dot{w}}{w} - \phi) \\
& \frac{\dot{w}}{w} = -\gamma + \rho\frac{L}{N} \\
& S = S(y) \\
& M^d = F(p, y, r) \\
& p(I - S) + \eta(M^d - M) = 0.
\end{aligned}
\qquad [2.18]
$$

The notation is the same as the one used in the Goodwin growth cycle model. In the investment equation the availability of credit in the economy, owing to the existence of a banking system, is considered in addition to profits. Formally this variable is expressed as the difference between the growth rate of the money supply θ and the growth rate of income $\dot{y}/y$, with μ being the income elasticity of the money demand coefficient.

The equation for the growth rate of prices $\dot{p}/p$ is rather interesting: it is based on the Keynesian assumption that prices are determined with a "mark-up" over costs, with the additional assumption, drawn from Sylos-Labini, that the growth rate of prices is lower than the discrepancy between the growth rate of money wages and the growth rate of productivity[20] - that is, coefficient $\beta/(1+\beta)$ is less than unity. The assumption implies that average profits increase when costs are decreasing whereas they decrease when costs are increasing.

The third equation is a linearised Phillips curve similar to the one employed in Goodwin (1967); the fourth is the Keynesian function relating savings S to income. The next is a money demand equation, in which the money demand M^D is positively related to prices and income, and negatively to the interest rate r. Finally, the equilibrium condition for the whole system is stated, according to which any discrepancy between investment and savings is compensated by a discrepancy, of the opposite sign, between the flows of money demand and money supply.

In the model the *monetary* sector constitutes a sub-system and hence it may be dealt with separately from the *real* side. The latter may be reduced to a system of two differential equations of the Lotka-Volterra type in the two variables $v \equiv L/N$ and $u \equiv wL/pX$, the solution of which gives rise to closed orbits around the equilibrium point, similar to the ones in the Goodwin model, as is illustrated in Figure (2.9).

Once again, at the stationary solution (point T of the diagram) given from the condition: $\dot{u}=0$ and $\dot{v}=0$, the employment rate is $v \equiv c/\rho$ [21], and the system grows at the natural rate, $\dot{y}/y=\phi+n$, equal to the sum of the growth rate of productivity ϕ and the growth rate of the labour supply n, with zero

---

20 Cf. P. Sylos-Labini (1967), where the assumption is explained with the oligopolistic structure of markets. Oligopoly makes firms reluctant to change prices in the same proportion as the variation in costs, to avoid curbing the expansion of total demand and for fear of a decrease in each firm's market share due to the entry of competitors.

21 In this model $c = (\beta+\phi)/(1+\beta)$; $\rho=\theta/(1+\beta)$. (Cf. Di Matteo (1984)).

inflation and employment below full employment. One difference with the basic Goodwin model is that, now, the rate of profit and the profit-share are influenced by the value of the growth rate of the money supply, θ. The higher θ is, the lower the rate of profit and the profit share are.

When the system is out of the steady-state equilibrium, it moves along the trajectories of the closed orbits, each corresponding to a given set of initial conditions. Each orbit describes a full cycle, from the trough *P*, where the employment rate v is at its lowest level, to the peak *P'*, where v is at its highest level.

In *P* and *P'* there is equilibrium between investment and savings, whereas in *Q* and *Q'* there is a positive and negative discrepancy, respectively, between the two variables.

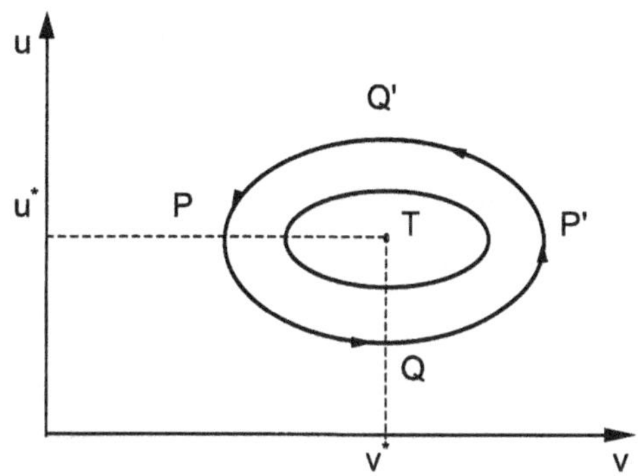

Figure 2.9. *Closed orbits in the Di Matteo model*

In the *P-Q* segment the low level of the employment rate v leads money wages to grow more slowly than productivity. This makes profits, accumulation and, consequently, income grow, while the growth rate of prices is negative – according to the second equation of system [2.18]. The system is, therefore, in the early stages of the expansion process. In Q the growth rate of money wages equals the growth rate of productivity, so that inflation is zero.

The increase in income and employment beyond v^* leads to a steady increase in the bargaining power of the labour force, thus pushing the growth rate of money wages beyond the growth rate of productivity. Hence, between Q and P' there is a slowdown in the accumulation process due to the fall in profits, and positive inflation: the system is in the late stages of the expansion.

As Di Matteo himself points out, the factors driving the dynamics of the system in this reformulation of the Goodwin model are still the ones emphasized by Goodwin in his basic model, that is, variables v and u. Monetary quantities appearing in the Di Matteo model do not change the results substantially, because of the lack of a true interdependence between the *real* and *monetary* sides[22].

Finally, the author analyses the role of monetary policy within this setting. When θ equals the natural growth rate, the model has the same origin as the Goodwin model, although fluctuations are smaller in amplitude. Moreover, as θ decreases the amplitude of fluctuations decreases, too, and vice-versa.

As to the role of a counter-cyclical monetary policy, the degree of endogeneity of money influences its effectiveness. In particular, a contraction of the money supply may stop the expansion, changing the trajectory of the system so that point P' moves to the left, towards the centre T. On the other hand, an expansion of the money supply not directed towards the encouragement of

22 The author stresses that two conditions need to be fulfilled for the dynamics of the rate of interest and of accumulation being consistent. In the long run, the rate of interest should not exceed the rate of profit, because it allows the repayment of debt out of realised profits, thus keeping up the incentive to invest. Secondly, the rate of interest should not deviate too much from the real rate of profit, because that would reduce liquidity and increase its premium, thus inducing the postponement of investment in capital assets.

investment and the increase of employment could be insufficient to sustain the level of economic activity.

The Asada model

Asada (1989) extends the Goodwin growth cycle model by adding the monetary sector and considering the role of monetary policy in the analysis of fluctuations and instability. Once the model is reformulated to give it some Keynesians features, the main source of instability is to be found in the financial sector. Hence Asada investigates the mechanisms through which stability may be transmitted to the *real* side of the economy and the role of an "active" monetary policy aimed to contrast it.

First of all, a Keynesian investment function is adopted:

$$g = (r_n,\ i - \pi^*); \quad g_1 = \partial g / \partial r_n > 0, \quad g_2 = \partial g / \partial (i - \pi^*) < 0$$

where $g \equiv I/K$ is the accumulation rate, $r_n \equiv (1 - t_r)(pX - wL) / pK$ is the pre-tax profit rate, with t_r the average tax rate on profit income and $i\text{-}\pi^*$ the real interest rate, given by the difference between the monetary interest rate i and the rate of price inflation π^*.

The equilibrium condition in the goods market is then given by:

$$X = (1 - t_w)\omega L + (1 - s_r)(1 - t_r)(X - \omega L) + I + G$$

where t_w is the average wage-income tax, $\omega = w/p$ is the real wage, s_r is the capitalists' average propensity to save and G is real government expenditure.

For the purpose of carrying out the dynamic analysis of the model it is convenient to divide both sides of the equation by *K*. By substituting the corresponding expression for *g*, the following equation is obtained:

[2.19]:

$$\delta x^*[1-(1-s_r)(1-t_r)-\frac{s_r(1-t_r)+(t_r-t_w)}{1-t_w}Z_n]=g(\delta x^*(1-t_r)(1-\frac{1}{1-t_w}Z_n),\, i-\pi^*)+h,$$

where $\delta x^* \equiv X/K$ (with δ equal to the capacity utilisation ratio, between zero and one, and x^* equal to the capital-output ratio corresponding to the full utilisation of resources), $Z_n \equiv (1-t_w)wL/pX$ the pre-tax wage-share of income; and $h \equiv G/K$.

The LM equation for the money market equilibrium is:

$$M/P = X \cdot \phi(i,\, \pi^*); \quad \phi_1 \equiv \partial\phi/\partial i < 0; \quad \phi_2 \equiv \partial\phi/\partial\pi^* \leq 0,$$

where ϕ (..) is the reciprocal of the velocity of the circulation of money. If both sides of the equation are divided by *K*, the following is obtained:

$$m = \delta x^* \phi(i,\, \pi^*); \quad m \equiv M/pK. \qquad [2.20]$$

Having defined ℓ as the labour-capital ratio *L/K* and L^S as the supply of labour, the model is completed by adding seven more equations to the IS-LM system:

$$\dot{w}/w = f(E) + \pi^*; \; f'(E) > 0$$

$$E \equiv L / L^s \equiv \delta \ell x^* K / L^s$$
$$Z_n \equiv (1-t_w) wL / pX \equiv (1-t_w) w\ell / p$$
$$\pi \equiv \dot{p} / p$$
$$g(\delta x^* (1-t_r)(1-\frac{1}{1-t_w} Z_n, \; i-\pi^*) = \dot{K} / K$$
$$\dot{L}^s / L^s = n_1; \; n_1 \equiv \text{constant}$$
$$\dot{\ell} / \ell = -n_2; \; n_2 \equiv \text{constant.}$$

The first is an expectation-augmented Phillips curve relating workers' bargaining power to the rate of employment E; the following four equations define, respectively, the employment rate E, the pre-tax wage-share of total income Z_n , the rate of price inflation π and the increase in the stock of capital $\dot{K} / K$ through the flow of investment. The meaning of the last two equations is that the growth rates of the labour force $\dot{L}^S / L^S$ and of labour productivity $\dot{\ell} / \ell$ are constant and exogenously given.

The system is made up of nine independent equations and twelve unknown, or endogenous, variables: E, Z_n, p, w, π, π^*, i, K, L^S, ℓ, δ, M. There are three degrees of freedom and the way one chooses to "close" the system affects the nature of the resulting model. In particular, Asada shows that a Goodwin-type closure would mean adding the following three equations:

$$\delta = 1; \quad \pi = \pi^*; \quad \dot{M} / M = \mu + \alpha(i - \bar{i}), \quad \alpha \geq 0,$$

where the first states the full utilisation of the productive capacity, the second the perfect-foresight hypothesis, and the last gives the monetary policy rule. In particular, $\alpha = 0$ corresponds to a monetarist rule with a fixed growth rate of money supply (μ), whereas $\alpha > 0$ corresponds to a Keynesian rule.

The complete model of twelve equations may be reduced to the following more compact system:

$$\begin{aligned}
&(i)\ H(Z_n) = \tilde{g}(Z_n,\ i-\pi)+h \\
&(ii)\ m = x^*\phi(i,\ \pi) \\
&(iii)\ \dot{m}/m = \mu+\alpha(i-\bar{i})-\pi-\tilde{g}(Z_n,\ i-\pi) \\
&(iv)\ \dot{Z}_n/Z_n = (\dot{w}/w)-\pi-n_2 = f(E)-n_2 \\
&(v)\ \dot{E}/E = \tilde{g}(Z_n,\ i-\pi)-(n_1+n_2)
\end{aligned} \qquad [2.21]$$

where $H(Z_n) \equiv x^*[1-(1-s_r)(1-t_r)-\{s_r(1-t_r)+(t_r-t_w)\}Z_n/(1-t_w)]$; $\tilde{g}(Z_n, i-\pi) \equiv g(x^*(1-t_r)\{1-Z_n/(1-t_w)\}, i-\pi)$ and where Z_n, E, m, i and π are the endogenous variables.

The system has a classical nature as can be seen from the fact that the *real* side of the model is determined independently of the *monetary* side - that is, there is a dichotomy. In fact, given Z_n, E and m in the short run, the short-run equilibrium values of i and π are determined via equations [2.21i] and [2.21ii], so that the corresponding accumulation rate g attained is always the one which guarantees the full utilisation of resources by the adjustment of the real rate of interest, which is thus determined independently in the goods markets.

Moreover, by expressing equation [2.21i] in terms of the real interest rate $[(i-\pi) = \Phi(Z_n)]$ and using it to obtain equation [2.21ii] in terms of the rate of price inflation $[\pi = \pi(Z_n, m)]$, system [2.21] may be reduced further to the following fundamental system:

$$\begin{aligned}
&(i)\ \dot{Z}_n = \{f(E)-n_2\}Z_n \equiv F_1(Z_n,E) \\
&(ii)\ \dot{E} = \{H(Z_n)-(h+n_1+n_2)\}E \equiv F_2(Z_n,E) \\
&(iii)\ \dot{m} = \left[\mu+\alpha\{i(Z_n,m)-\bar{i}\}-\pi(Z_n,m)-H(Z_n)+h\right]m \equiv F_3(Z_n,m).
\end{aligned} \qquad [2.22]$$

It is evident that the first two equations of system [2.22] constitute a sub-system of two equations which can be solved in terms of the two endogenous Z_n and E, independently of the last equation. This sub-system may be analysed by means of the procedure employed for the Goodwin model (1967), and obtaining the solution of a closed orbit around the steady-state equilibrium point, for given initial conditions $[Z_n(0), E(0)]$ which will determine the amplitude of the cycle.

The behaviour of E, Z_n and $(i-\pi)$ over the cycle is sketched out in the diagram of Figure (2.10).

Asada proves[23] that monetary policy may be effective in stabilising the monetary variables, although it is ineffective in controlling the real variables.

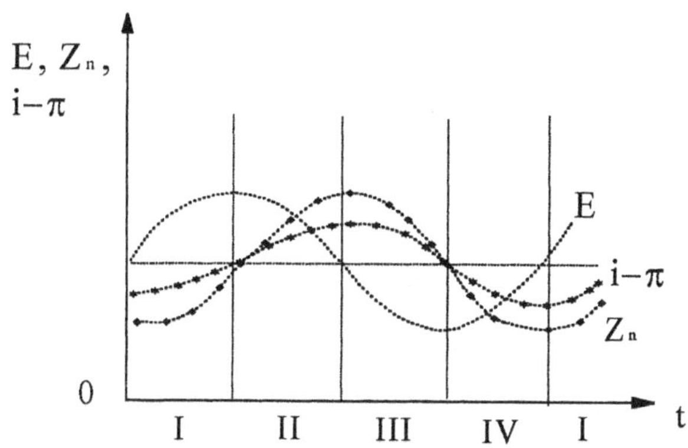

Figure 2.10. *The behaviour of the employment rate, real interest rate and wage-share over time in the Asada model*

After the linearisation of system [2.22] around the equilibrium point Z_n^*, E^*, m^*, the author obtains the following (approximate) solution to the system:

23 For analytical details, cf. T. Asada (1989), pp. 150–167.

$$(i)\ Z_n(t) = Z_n^* + B_1 \cos(\theta t + \varepsilon_1)$$
$$(ii)\ E(t) = E^* + B_2 \cos(\theta t + \varepsilon_2) \qquad [2.23]$$
$$(iii)\ m(t) = m^* + Ae^{\lambda_1 t} + B_3 \cos(\theta t + \varepsilon_3)$$

with $\lambda_1 \equiv (a-1)\pi_2 * m*$; $\theta \equiv \sqrt{-H'(Z_n*)f'(E*)Z_n * E*}$, and A and B_j (j = 1, 2, 3) constants depending on the initial conditions[24]. It is evident that for $a = 0$, corresponding to the monetarist rule, $\lambda_1 > 0$ so that the behaviour of m and consequently of π becomes explosive. On the other hand, for $a > 1$ the dynamics of the system is "tamed".

In a second stage of the work the author proves that changing the assumption about the capitalists' propensity to save, and making it a decreasing function of the expected inflation rate, that is, setting $s_r = s_r(\pi^*)$; $s_r'(\pi^*) < 0$, while keeping all the other variables constant, the dichotomy of the system disappears. Moreover, if the sensitivity of the capitalists' propensity to save with respect to the expected rate of inflation is sufficiently small, then the equilibrium solution appears to be unstable in the presence of a monetarist policy rule, whereas it would become stable with $a > 0$. Finally, the conditions are stated for the existence of a positive-valued range for parameter a at which cyclical fluctuations around the equilibrium point do not occur.

Another experiment by the author is the substitution of the assumption of perfect-foresight with the one of adaptive expectations, that is: $s_r = s_r(\pi^*)$; $s_r'(\pi^*) < 0$. The results obtained are that for small expectations coefficient γ and for large monetary policy parameter α, there exists a set of local stability conditions for the system.

---

24 Cf. Appendix A.5.

2.4 – Financial Dynamics and Business Cycles

Debt, financial fragility and systemic instability

The importance in the concrete working of modern capitalist economies of the financial system as a whole, that is, the set of its markets and intermediaries, necessarily calls for the extension of the analysis to the interrelations between money, finance and *real* activity, that is, production, investment, consumption and so on.

The different ways in which *financial* determinants have entered the study of cyclical fluctuations basically reflect the theoretical perspectives of the different approaches to the analysis of business cycles. In fact, within the recent Neo-classical setting of the *Equilibrium Business Cycle* modelling, monetary theories have been used, since Lucas (1981), to explain cycles as the result of the economic systems' responses to the continuous accidental exogenous monetary shocks to which they are subject. As mentioned in the Introduction, that kind of modelling is based on a rather stylised and simplified view of economic systems, which neglects the complex relationships that reflect the existence of sophisticated financial structures, and considers financial markets as perfect co-ordinators of investment and savings decisions. In that perspective, *financial* variables appear to be "neutral" with respect to the economic performance. Besides, economic performance could still be perfectly defined and explained by the behaviour of *real* variables alone, were external shocks absent. In the Keynesian modelling, instead, *financial* determinants play a fundamental role in the overall behaviour of the economic system, especially in the context of uncertainty and in the presence of co-ordination failures, which are typical of capitalist economies. *Financial* variables, in Keynesian analyses, interact with *real* variables, thus deeply affecting the behaviour of the economy.

Even in the early Fifties and Sixties, Gurley and Shaw had placed emphasis on the role of *financial* variables. With more specific reference to the *financial fragility* issue, some years later Minsky[25] focused on the definition of the mechanisms that regulate the endogenous determination of the accumulation process and of business fluctuations. In his work the stress was on the links between the investment decisions of a single firm and its financial structure, as indicated in particular by the ratio of internal funds (from retained profits) to debt, with a view to understanding, at the aggregate level, the dynamics of debt and, correspondingly, the behaviour of investment during the cycle.

Minsky's starting point was the two functions P_K and P_I that constitute, respectively, the demand price of capital goods, given by the capitalisation of the expected quasi-rents, and the supply price of new capital goods, which is equal to the minimum price required to produce an additional unit of that good. By making use of the Keynesian terminology, Minsky modified the two functions in order to take account of the *borrower risk* and the *lender risk*[26],

25 This is a theoretical issue which goes back to the seminal contribution by I. Fisher (1933), the study of which has recently stimulated renewed attention and received great impulse with H. P. Minsky (1975). More recently, some authors have drawn on the so-called *Economics of Information* literature in order to provide microeconomic foundations to the *financial fragility* hypothesis. On this point, see also the contributions by D. Delli Gatti – M. Gallegati – L. Gardini (1993) and D. Delli Gatti – M. Gallegati (1994).

26 The *borrower* risk is due, firstly, to the circumstance that risk-adverse investors diversify their portfolio, under conditions of uncertainty, and secondly, to the decrease in the margins of safety (for the firm) with increasing levels of investment, because of the *certain* nature of expected outflows and the *uncertain* nature of the expected inflows. Both factors lead to a decrease in the capitalisation rate on expected returns, with the result that as investment increases the *borrower* risk also increases, and the price of capital goods falls from its original level. The fall of prices is larger the higher the "leverage" ratio of the firm. The *lender* risk, instead, increases with the increase in the ratio between outside funds and inside funds of the firm, and it appears in terms of higher interest rates on lending, binding repayment conditions, collateral. It reduces the flexibility in the financial and economic management of the firm. The cost of investment, therefore, is determined by adding to the price P_I the increasing financial costs associated with the increasing *lender* risk.

which are related, respectively, to the probability that the firm realises the expected income, and to the voluntary or involuntary non-fulfilment of the obligation.

Keynes had highlighted that, generally, during expansions the evaluation of both risks becomes imprudently low. According to Minsky, firms find themselves with an unutilised margin of "borrowing capacity" that determines a shift in the leverage considered acceptable. This is a stimulus to the expansion of investment supported by debt.

At the aggregate level, the amount of internal finance is a function of the level of investment, that is, of aggregate income. Higher levels of internal funds encourage investment, by the use of the firms' available borrowing-capacity margins. Therefore, the leverage of the system increases steadily, up to the point that the fulfilment of the debt contracts requires an inflow of liquidity which is faster than the one generated through the firm's business. Hence, in these circumstances the increase in the default-risk leads to further binding conditions on financial markets, which may accelerate a liquidity crisis and determine debt-deflation.

According to Minsky, in the early stage of an expansion the banking system accommodates the growing demand for liquidity in the system. Nevertheless, as the expansion supported by debt proceeds, the *systemic* risk increases because of the *financial fragility* of firms. The supply of finance, then, becomes progressively inelastic, up to the point that the refusal of banking credit forces firms to sell off their assets, thus letting prices fall.

Expansion is followed by a fall in investment, and the system is driven into a recession, with agents recreating the financial and economic equilibria which have been compromised by the euphoria of easy indebtedness and precipitous realisations on financial markets.

Hence, an endogenous mechanism is at work in the determination of the financial structure, which is closely related to the cyclical behaviour of the economy. Indeed, a stable financial structure, that is, one in which *hedge* finance units predominate, gives an incentive to debt-financed investment, thus leading to a progressive deterioration of the financial structure of firms. They become *speculative* finance units when the discrepancy between inflows and outflows is referred to the short run and *Ponzi* or *ultra-speculative* when the discrepancy is of such an entity that firms have to increase their borrowing even further in order to fulfil debt commitments, thus increasing the overall risk and instability.

More recently, the New Keynesians have placed emphasis on the financial fragility issue, also on the basis of empirical support to the assumption that *financial* factors, and especially debt, are of particular relevance to economic performance[27]. The renewed interest in this topic has stimulated theoretical research at the macroeconomic level, too, in particular with regard to business cycles. A very important contribution in this direction comes from the theoretical developments on the working of capital markets, and in particular credit markets, by the *Economics of Information and Incentives* approach. This has provided solid microeconomic underpinnings to the analysis of the real-financial interaction[28]. The basic idea is the following. Were capital markets

---

27 F. Minshkin (1978) and B. Bernanke (1983) found empirical evidence of the role played by the deterioration of firms' financial structures – due to the high level of debt and to the lending conditions – on aggregate demand during the Great Depression. Empirical works concerned with the financial nature of cycles are in B. Friedman (1980), (1982), where a greater stability of the debt-output ratio was found in comparison with the money-output ratio. An empirical investigation on the relationship between financial fragility and systemic instability during the cycle is in C. Niggle (1989) and M. Wolfson (1989).

28 See M. Gertler (1988) for a survey of the literature. For further specific reference, cf. B. S. Bernanke – M. Gertler (1987), (1990); A. Blinder – J. E. Stiglitz (1983); and also B. Greenwald – J. Stiglitz – A. Weiss (1984) and B. Greenwald – J. Stiglitz (1993) who examine the macroeconomic effects of equity rationing. In B. Greenwald – J. Stiglitz (1990), then, the roles of both credit and equity market are investigated.

frictionless and perfectly competitive, then it would always be possible to consider the different types of finance as homogeneous goods, and to consider capital as a unique *fluid* which moves from one side to the other of the economic system seeking the highest earnings, and following the indications coming from the market interest rates.

Yet, because of imperfect information and incomplete markets, rationing equilibria may occur which are Pareto sub-optimal. In that case, systematic biases in the allocation of resources might act against the undertaking of *good quality* projects – as opposed to *bad quality* projects. In addition to the allocative effects, consequences at the aggregate level could be present, too. For instance, total investment expenditure will depend on the way "adverse selection" and "adverse incentive" problems affect the individual investment decisions. If the increase in investment expenditure by those who benefit from the aforementioned distortions in the allocation of funds is less then the decrease by those who are damaged from them, then the overall result will be a negative performance of aggregate investment.

A common result of this modelling is that investment by firms as well as production decisions depend largely on credit conditions, both in *quantity* and *price* terms. Binding financial constraints may lead to external funds being available in less then the desired amount - that is, they may have a *liquidity effect* - and/or they may make it impossible to achieve the desired financial structure because of a high marginal cost of external finance – that is, they may have a *cost effect.* In this respect, some models emphasize that the market equilibrium level of investment is closely linked to the financial position in assets and liabilities of economic units, which is indicated by the equity-debt ratio. A low level of that ratio, suggesting a low degree of financial independence, may in some circumstances compromise the financial "governance" of the firm, and determine increasing costs of external financing[29]. Markets evaluate positively a high degree of internal funds, because it constitutes a form of guarantee for lenders; hence, it reduces the *effective marginal cost* of capital for firms. In this case, the financial structure is not irrelevant for investment and production decisions, contrary to the Modigliani-Miller theorem.

The importance of theoretical issues typical of the earlier Keynesian tradition, such as the links between debt, financial fragility and systemic risk, emerges clearly. The Minsky hypothesis on the existence of a positive correlation between cash-flows and investment decisions of firms is reinforced further if the possibility of imperfections in financial markets is allowed for, as in the New Keynesian literature. An improvement in the firm's cash flow strengthens its financial structure. In the presence of information problems, this acts as an indicator of the risk faced by lenders and gives a positive *signal* to the market, thus reducing the *effective* cost of capital to the firm with positive feed backs to investment.

Because fluctuations in cash flows are closely linked to the economic performance, it is possible to envisage a cyclical interaction between the financial structure of firms and the behaviour of *real* variables, in which

29 On the basis of similar arguments, S. H. Fazzari – R. G. Hubbard – B. C. Petersen (1988) emphasized the existence of a *pecking order* or *financing hierarchy* of the different types of finance for firms. Internal funds have a lower opportunity-cost than debt, and the latter appear to be less onerous than equity capital. The authors find empirical evidence for this thesis in the data referring to the U.S. manufacturing firms, ranked on the basis of their profit-retention policies. The results are that the investment decisions of firms, especially those with a high retention-ratio, which use up almost all their internal funds and have a rather inelastic financial structure, are strongly affected by fluctuations in cash flows. This happens more easily during periods in which problems from imperfect information become relevant and liquidity constraints are binding. For firms which are mature and well-known to the market these kinds of problems should be less relevant and there should be no considerable difference in the opportunity cost of various types of finance.

imperfections in financial markets act as the propagating mechanism of the disturbances in the economic system.

Clearly, many of the assumptions and conclusions that economists have long been accustomed to are now under debate. For instance, the *representative firm* model is being criticised because markets are not indifferent to *who* the borrower is. Related to this is the assumption that the only relevant variable for investment decisions is given by the price signals which are set in well-behaved and frictionless capital markets.

Studies on debt, financial markets and economic performance within the context of business cycles analyses have taken advantage of the economic applications of the theory of dynamic systems, in particular, the recent developments in the theory of non-linear oscillations[30].

It is immediately possible to distinguish a group of macrodynamic models in which this issue is analysed in terms of the existence of exogenous constraints on the financing of firms' investment decisions. Financing constraints are, ultimately, the source of fluctuations in business activity during the cycle[31].

In other models, however, in particular in Foley (1986) and (1987), debt is determined endogenously, together with the production of investment goods by firms, the rate of profit and the overall liquidity of the system. The cyclical behaviour is the result of an unstable accelerator and a stabilising effect of liquidity, which is scarce in periods of high growth rates of income whereas it is abundant in periods of recession.

In Taylor and O'Connel (1985) the equity and the debt markets are introduced within an IS-LM framework. Agents' decisions as to the composition

---

30 On this point, cf. M. Hirsch – S. Smale (1974), T. Guckenheimer – P. Holmes (1983), G. Gandolfo (1996). For specific reference to the theory of chaotic dynamics, cf. D. Ruelle – F. Takens (1971), T. Li – J. Yorke (1975), A. Lasota – M. Mackey (1985).

31 See, e.g. M. Woodford (1986), (1988).

of the portfolio depend on the behaviour of profit rates and market interest rates. Both variables are closely linked to the economic performance during the cycle. The authors highlight the possibilities of complex dynamics emerging from the interaction between portfolio decisions and the behaviour of *real* markets.

Franke-Semmler (1989) developed this approach, making the role of indebtedness and financial commitments of firms in determining macroeconomic fluctuations more explicit[32].

The Franke-Semmler model

As in Taylor O' Conell (1985), an "enlarged" non-linear IS-LM framework is considered, with two markets, the goods and the asset markets, the firms which make investment decisions, the *rentiers* who save part of the profits accruing from firms, the banking system and the public sector. The debt of firms is made completely endogenous to the model and its behaviour over time feeds back to the investment decisions, through its influence on the anticipated net profitability, the demand for finance, the assets markets and the interest rates.

First of all, the variables are defined as follows. The gross rate of profit $r^g = \dfrac{PX - W}{P_K K}$ where P is the price of real output X, W is total wages to workers, K the stock of physical capital of the firms and P_K its price. The net rate of profit $r = \dfrac{PX - W - iD}{P_K K}$, with D as the stock of firms' debt with banks, and i the interest rate on loans. Setting: $\lambda = D / P_K K$, the following relationship between the two rates of profit holds: $r^g = r + i\lambda$.

32 The 1989 model is presented here since in this pioneering contribution the basic question of the relationship between the liquidity creation process, debt and financial fragility in a growth model is already dealt with in a very clear and tractable way. A further step in the theoretical modelling of the *real-financial* interaction was taken by the authors in their more recent 1994 work.

The demand price of capital goods P_K is determined on the basis of the capitalisation of the flow of expected profits per unit of investment, that is: $P_K = \frac{r^g + \rho}{i} P$, where ρ is the difference between the expected and the current profit rates, and it identifies the "state of confidence" of firms. The determination of the share prices P_E is given by the budget constraint of the firms: $P_e E = P_K K - D$.

The analysis is performed in two stages. Initially, the authors examine the working of the goods and of the asset markets in the short run, finding the equilibrium values of the interest rate, the gross and the net profit rates and the growth rate of the stock of capital as functions of the leverage ratio λ and of the state of confidence ρ. The motion of this two variables is then analysed, on the basis of the results obtained in the first stage.

In order to obtain the portfolio equilibrium condition, corresponding to the LM equation, Franke and Semmler draw up a prospect in which the assets and liabilities positions of all economic units are identified, that is, of firms, *rentiers*, commercial banks and the Central Bank, as illustrated in Table (2.1).

The prospect shows that net wealth W equals the base money F plus the value of the stock of capital, $P_K K$. The demand for deposits $d_0 = d_0 = (r+\rho, i)$ and the demand for equities $e = e(r+\rho, i)$ are set as functions of the expected rate of profit $r + \rho$, and of the rate of interest i. The *rentiers'* preferences as to the composition of net wealth W is expressed as: $D_0 = d_0 W$; $D_i = (1 - d_0 - e)W$; $P_e E = eW$.

It is assumed that the Monetary Authorities control the credit multiplier $\mu > 1$, and that the following holds: $(D_0 + D_i)/D_c = \mu$. The reciprocal of the velocity of the base money with respect to the stock of capital is a given constant, $\phi = F/PK$, where for simplicity, $P_K = P$.

Table 2.1

	Assets			Liabilities
Central Bank				
	High-powered money	F	D_c	Deposits of commercial banks
Commercial Banks	Bank reserves	D_c	D_o	Interest-free deposit from the public
	Loans to firms	D	D_i	Interest-bearing dep. from the public
Firms				
	Capital stock (valued at the demand price)	P_kK	D	Loans from commercial banks
			P_eE	Equity
Public ("rentiers")	Deposit with commercial banks	D_o D_i	W	Wealth
Equity		P_eE		

By combining the above relations and by taking into account the two conditions[33] $P_E/PK = (r+\rho)/i$ and $\mu F = \mu D_c = (1 - e)W$, the asset market equilibrium condition is easily obtained[34]:

$$e - \frac{r+\rho}{r+\rho+i(\lambda+\phi)} = 0. \qquad [2.24]$$

As for the goods markets, following Kalecki, investment decisions are set as a function of the difference between the anticipated return on holding capital and the rate of interest:

33 For analytical details, see R. Franke – W. Semmler (1989), pp. 40-43.

34 The policy variables μ and ϕ and the indebtedness ratio λ are linked by the following constraint: $(\mu - 1)\phi - \lambda = 0$. Because of the constancy of ϕ the asset market condition implies that μ adjusts continuously to satisfy the above constraint.

$$PI = h\, PK, \qquad h' = dh / d(r + \rho - i) > 0.$$

Having defined *PG* as the public deficit, and assuming that it is financed only by the creation of base money, so that $PG = \dot{F}$, the following holds:

$$\text{(i)}\ PG = \phi\ PI.$$

Hence, the equilibrium condition between demand and supply implies that:

$$\text{(ii)}\ PC + PI + PG = PX = W + r^{g} PK.$$

By taking into account the assumption of a Kalecki-type savings function, so that workers consume entirely their income, it follows that: $PS = s r^{g} PK$, where s is the propensity to save of the *rentiers*. By combining the above relations, the expression for the IS equation is easily obtained:

$$(1+ \phi)\, h\, (r + \rho - i) - s\ r^{g} = 0. \qquad [2.25]$$

At this point, stage two of the analysis is undertaken, by introducing the dynamics through the laws of motion of the two variables: the ratio of indebtedness λ, and the *state of confidence* ρ, which enter into the determination of the "temporary" equilibria of the goods and assets markets.

As far as the rate of indebtedness is concerned, a high value of it increases the default-risk of firms, because of the difficulties in the fulfilment of debt commitments through the realised flow of current profits. The motion of debt is therefore described by the law:

$$\dot{D}/D = b(r^g + \rho - i, \lambda)$$

and, because of the above considerations, the signs of the partial derivatives are:

$$b_r = \partial b / \partial(r^g + \rho - i) \geq 0; \quad b_\lambda = \partial b / \partial \lambda \leq 0.$$

Since $\dot{\lambda}/\lambda = \dot{D}/D - \dot{K}/K$, if P is assumed to be constant and the equation for the growth rate of the capital stock is reformulated as $g = h\ (r + \rho - i)$, then the following law of motion of λ is obtained:

$$\dot{\lambda} = \lambda[b(r_g + \rho - i, \lambda) - g]. \tag{2.26}$$

As for the "state of expectations", it is assumed that the behaviour over time of the variable ρ is governed by the following law of motion:

$$\dot{\rho} = v[(r - i), \lambda], \tag{2.27}$$

where the two arguments denote, respectively, the liquidity position and the default-risk of the firms. The signs of the partial derivatives are:

$$v_r = \partial v / \partial(r - i) > 0; \quad v_\lambda = \partial v / \partial \lambda \leq 0.$$

By adding the laws of motion of λ and ρ (equations [2.26] and [2.27]) to equations [2.24] and [2.25] (the LM and IS equations, respectively), a system of four equations is obtained which may be solved in terms of the four unknown variables, r, i, λ and ρ, given the formula: $r^g = r + i\lambda$.

The analysis is carried out sequentially. First of all, the temporary equilibrium is obtained with respect to given λ and ρ, by solving the IS and LM equations in terms of the values of the net profit rate r and the interest rate i which clear the goods and the assets markets instantaneously. Hence, a sequence of changes in λ and ρ will bring about a sequence of new (temporary) equilibrium values for r and i which, accordingly, will feed back to λ and ρ.

Therefore, the overall dynamics of the system is described through a sequence of "temporary" equilibria, and for $\dot{\lambda}=0$ and $\dot{\rho}=0$ the change in r and i will cease and the system will find itself in a long-run equilibrium of steady growth. Lastly the authors analyse some alternative scenarios which emerge by considering different assumptions on the reaction functions of the model. In particular, in two cases there is a local stability with respect to a unique long-run equilibrium with steady growth, whereas a third case exhibits persistent fluctuations in all the variables involved, fluctuations which tend to a limit-cycle, that is, the system features cyclical growth.

CHAPTER III

The Role of Real Factors in Economic Fluctuations. A Basic Set Up

3.1 – Preface

The present Chapter develops a basic structure for a growth cycle model, in which the monetary side is treated in a simplified and "traditional" way, whereas the following Chapter presents an extension of the basic framework allowing for the consideration of the issues of firms' indebtedness, endogenous liquidity creation and financial fragility.

The work aims to highlight the interaction of *real* and *financial* determinants of business fluctuations in the economic process. As mentioned in the survey of the literature in Chapter II, the role of *real* factors emerges, on the one hand, in the Kalecki (1971), Kaldor (1940) and Goodwin (1951) models; on the other, in a class of models starting from the Goodwin (1967) growth cycle framework, up to the subsequent extensions by Di Matteo (1984) and Asada (1989). In the first case, the source of fluctuations is mainly due to the existence of disequilibrium in the goods markets; in the second case, fluctuations are basically governed by the dynamic interaction of income distribution and the employment rate. The role of *financial* determinants is explored in one class of models in the literature in which the contribution by Franke-Semmler (1989) stands out in particular. This approach draws on Minsky's analysis of financial fragility and the associated issues of liquidity creation, via the banking system, and debt as driving forces in the cycle.

In Section 3.2 the short-run features of the basic model I are described in the form of a basic, or "traditional", IS-LM framework. In Section 3.3 the dynamics is introduced by adding to the short-run system derived previously in Section 3.2 the laws of motion for the exogenous variables which are required in order to "close" the system. The dynamic model is thus complete. The dynamic features of the model are then investigated, followed by some comments on the results of the analysis.

3.2 – The Short-Run Equilibrium within a "Traditional" IS-LM Framework

At this stage of the analysis the attention is focused on the *real* side of the model, leaving the "traditional" analysis for the monetary side: the issues concerning the financing of investments and the dynamics of indebtedness are ignored, and emphasis is placed on the role of income distribution and the market structure as basic determinants of the behaviour of the economy.

The model is structured as a closed economy with two types of agents, the workers and the capitalists (*rentiers*). Following Kalecki (1954) it is assumed, for the sake of simplicity, that workers consume all their income, in the form of wages, whereas capitalists spend in consumption only part of their income, in the form of profits accruing from the firms. The latter make the investment decisions.

The *real* side of the model is described by the following equations. First of all, real income, real wages and the rate of profit are defined by the following identities (i)-(iii):

(i) $X \equiv W + \Pi$

(ii) $W \equiv (w/p)\,N$

(iii) $r \equiv \dfrac{\Pi}{K} \equiv \dfrac{\Pi}{X} \cdot \dfrac{X}{K}$

where in (i), total real output X is distributed between total real wages W and total real profits Π; in (ii) w/p is the real wage accruing to workers and N is the level of employment; in (iii) r is the current rate of profit, defined as the ratio of total real profits Π to the stock of capital K. The rate of profit may also be expressed as the product of the two ratios appearing on the right hand side of (iii), that is, the profit-share Π/X and the output-capital ratio X/K.

Given the aforesaid Kaleckian assumption on the behaviour of workers and capitalists, the consumption function results in the following:

$$\begin{aligned} C &= (w/p)N + c_\pi \Pi \\ &= W + c_\pi \Pi, \qquad 0 < c_\pi < 1 \end{aligned} \qquad [3.1']$$

where c_π denotes the capitalists' propensity to consume out of real profits.

Firms' investment decisions are described by the function:

$$I = I^o + \gamma[r^e - (i - \pi^e)]K, \qquad \gamma' > 0$$

where $I°$ is the autonomous component and $\gamma[...]$ is a function representing the economic incentive to invest, measured by the difference between the anticipated profitability of investment r^e and the real rate of interest $(i - \pi^e)$, with π^e equal to the expected rate of price inflation.

The investment equation may be reformulated by expressing the expected rate of profit as the sum of the current profit rate r and its expected change ρ, that is, by setting $r^e = r + \rho$, thus leading to:

$$I = I^o + \gamma[(r + \rho) - (i - \pi^e)]K. \qquad [3.2']$$

The (anticipated) difference between the expected profit rate r^e and the current profit rate r, denoted as ρ, is the variable used as the measure of the "state of confidence" of firms[1]. In the short run its value is assumed to be given; its behaviour over time and the role it plays in the accumulation process and in the macroeconomic performance will be considered in Section 3.3, in the analysis of the long run equilibrium and the dynamics of the model.

Equation [3.2'] asserts that investment decisions are made on the basis of the *expected relative profitability* of investment in new capital goods, according to the traditional assumption in Keynesian modelling that investment is a function of the difference between the marginal efficiency of capital and its (replacement) cost. A reformulation in terms of percentage rates, rather then of levels, may be deduced by Minsky's theory of investment. As recalled in the survey in Chapter II, Minsky makes investment depend on the difference between the demand price P_K and the supply price P_I of new capital goods.

1 This function is similar to the one employed in R. Franke – W. Semmler (1989), where the expected rate of price inflation π^e is not considered. On the other hand, T. Asada (1989) assumes investment to depend on the difference between the current rate of profit and the real rate of interest, and hence, does not take into consideration the role of changes in expectations about profitability. In the present work, as will be explained at length in the following section, the consideration of the "state of confidence" of the firms is one way in which the role of aggregate demand and capacity utilisation are introduced into the analysis.

Then, following Minsky, the demand price is given by the capitalisation of the expected quasi-rents per unit of investment, and by using the notation already introduced, it may be expressed as:

$$P_K = (r + \rho)\, p / i\,.$$

And if it is assumed that $P_I = p$, to simplify, the difference between the demand price and the supply price is:

$$P_K - p = [(r + \rho)\, p / i] - p\,,$$

$$P_K - p = [(r + \rho - i)\, p]/i.$$

From the last relation it is possible to get an expression for the investment demand function in real terms[2]:

$$I = I^o + [\gamma(r + \rho - i)]K\,.$$

The remaining equations of the *real* side are briefly commented below.

To simplify as far as possible, the level of employment is assumed to be proportional to the level of output:

$$N = (1/x)\, X\,, \qquad [3.3']$$

where x is the average productivity of labour (X/N).

The price equation is specified following Kalecki (1954), again. It is assumed that prices are determined on the basis of a *mark-up* over costs:

2 See also L. Taylor – S. O' Connel (1985); W. Semmler (1989).

$$p = m\,(w/x), \qquad m > 1 \tag{3.4}$$

where m is the "*mark-up* factor", given in the short-run, which in Kalecki represented the "degree of monopoly" power enjoyed by firms.

In particular, the *mark-up* factor defines the distribution of income between real wages and real profits. In fact, if equations [3.3'] and [3.4] are taken into account, it is possible to express the two income-shares in terms of the *mark-up* factor:

$$W/X \equiv (w/p)(N/X) = \{w/\,[m\,(w/x)]\}\,(1/x);$$
$$\Pi/X \equiv 1 - W/X,$$

which lead to:

$$W/X = (1/m);$$
$$\Pi/X = (1 - 1/m).$$

Finally, the real side of the (short-run) model is completed by adding the equation which states the equilibrium condition between demand and supply in the goods markets:

$$X = C + I + A \tag{3.5'}$$

where A represents the autonomous component of expenditure.

In the short run the money-wage is given. It may be considered as corresponding to the level of the *reservation wage*, or set on the basis of the bargaining between workers and firms, as in the *New Keynesian* modelling.

Hence, the money-wage w as well as the "state of confidence" ρ and the labour productivity x are exogenous variables from a short-run point of view. The distribution of income is given, too – given the *mark-up* factor m.

The monetary-side of the model is described by the money market equilibrium condition which is of a "traditional" Keynesian type:

$$M/p = h\,(X, i), \qquad h'_y > 0 \text{ and } h'_i < 0, \qquad [3.6']$$

where M is the money supply and $h(..)$ is the demand for money function in real terms, which is supposed to be directly related to the level of real income, in consideration of the transaction component, and inversely related to the interest rate, in view of the *speculative* component concerning the choice between holding money or bonds yielding the market interest rate i.

If relations (i)-(iii) are substituted into the first five equations above the resulting system of six equations may be solved to get the short-run equilibrium values of the model.

At this point the six equations of the short-run system can be reformulated to allow for the dynamic analysis of the following section. If both sides of equations [3.1'] – [3.6'] are divided by K, except for equation [3.4], of course, the following system is obtained:

$$C/K = (w/p)\,N/K + c_\pi\,[(X - (w/p)N]/K \qquad [3.1]$$

$$I/K = I°/K + \gamma[((X - (w/p)\,N)/K + \rho) - (i - \pi^e)] \qquad [3.2]$$

$$N/K = (1/x)\,X/K \qquad [3.3]$$

$$p = m\,(w/x) \qquad [3.4]$$

$$X/K = C/K + I/K + A/K \qquad [3.5]$$

$$M/pK = h\,(X/K, i) \qquad [3.6]$$

where the endogenous variables are: N/K, X/K, p, C/K, I/K, i, and the exogenous variables are: $w, \rho, \pi^e, A, M, K, x, m$.

The system thus obtained may be reduced to the IS and LM equations, which give the equilibrium conditions for the goods and the money market, respectively. The IS equation is:

$$X/K=[(1/m)\ X/K + c_\pi(1\text{-}1/m)\ X/K] + \{I°/K + \gamma[(1\text{-}1/m)\ X/K + \rho - (i - \pi^e)]\} + A/K$$

which may be rearranged in the following way:

$$[(1 - c_\pi)(1\text{-}1/m)]\ X/K = I°/K + \gamma[(1\text{-}1/m)\ X/K + \rho - (i - \pi^e)] + A/K;$$

$$s\ (1\text{-}1/m)\ X/K = I°/K + \gamma[(1\text{-}1/m)\ X/K + \rho - (i - \pi^e)] + A/K \qquad \text{[E1]}$$

where $s = (1 - c_\pi)$ is the capitalists' propensity to save.

The expression for the LM equation is:

$$M/K = [m\ (w/x)]\ h(X/K, i). \qquad \text{[E2]}$$

Let us set $y \equiv X/K$, to make notation simple, and calculate the slope of the two curves, first, by taking a linear approximation of equations [E1] and [E2] around the equilibrium point, that is, at $X/K \equiv y = y^*$ and $i = i^*$ and, then, by proceeding to obtain the following two expressions:

$$\text{(a)}\quad \left.\frac{di}{dy}\right|_{IS} = [\ s(1\text{-}1/m) - \gamma'\ (1\text{-}1/m)]\ /\ (-\ \gamma') = -\ [(s - \gamma')\ (1\text{-}1/m)]\ /(\ \gamma')$$

(b) $\left.\dfrac{di}{dy}\right|_{LM} = -\dfrac{h_y^{'}}{h_i^{'}}.$

Since $\gamma' > 0$, expression (a) is negative or positive depending on $(s - \gamma')$ being positive or negative, respectively. Hence, given the value of m and, consequently, the (short-run) distribution of income between wages and profits, the IS curve is downward sloping if the capitalists' propensity to save s is greater than the sensitivity of investment decisions to the expected profitability γ'. Moreover, the smaller the profit-share $\Pi/X = (1\text{-}1/m)$ is, the flatter the IS curve is.

As to the LM curve, because of the assumptions on the income sensitivity and the interest sensitivity of the demand for money function, that is $h_y^{'} > 0$ and $h_i^{'} < 0$, respectively, the sign of expression (b) is always positive, and so the LM curve is upward sloping.

Further analytical details with some results and comments on the comparative static properties regarding the short-run system can be found in Appendix B.

3.3 – Long-Run Equilibrium and Dynamics

In the analysis of the preceding section time does not enter in an essential way into the functions which characterise the short-run equilibrium of the model. As explained at the beginning of the present Chapter, the IS-LM framework leads to a short-run equilibrium which constitutes a Keynesian equilibrium, in the sense that the corresponding level of income attained is one which guarantees equilibrium between savings and investment. It is not relevant *per se*, but as a link of the long-run sequence.

When moving to the dynamic analysis of the model it is necessary to specify the equations that give the laws of motion for all the variables involved in the model which in the short-run analysis are considered as exogenous, since they are inherited from the past: w, ρ, π^e, A, K, M, x, m. By adding the laws of motion for these variables, they are made endogenous and their time path is determined by the solution of the complete dynamic system, together with the time paths of the other variables which depend on them. By introducing the aforesaid "closing" equations to the system, *time* is allowed to enter significantly into the analysis. In other words, the model is made dynamic. Therefore, the next step of the analysis is to explain the laws of motion of these variables.

Following the Keynesian tradition in dynamic modelling, it is assumed that the motion of money-wages over time is governed by the law implicit in the Phillips curve, according to which increasing money-wages are associated with increasing rates of employment. This assumption is present in many reformulations of business cycle theory which refer more or less directly to the basic Goodwin model (1967). As explained in the survey, the latter refers more precisely to the Marxian theory of the business cycle, which is based on the conflict between workers and capitalists and on the notions of "industrial reserve army" and "exploitation".

Here, the following expectation-augmented formulation of the Phillips curve is adopted:

$$\dot{w}/w = f(N/N^S) + \dot{\pi}^e, \qquad f' > 0, \qquad [3.7]$$

where N^S is the supply of labour and the ratio N/N^S is the rate of employment.

As to *m*, the mark-up factor representing the degree of monopoly power enjoyed by the firms in the Kaleckian perspective, it may be assumed that its behaviour over time is linked, fundamentally, to the performance of wages and productivity during the cycle. One way of modelling this relation was suggested by Sylos-Labini (1967) in the analysis of the determination of the price level and its variation, within the context of imperfectly competitive markets. The author's point was that the mark-up decreases when money wages grow faster than productivity, and vice-versa.

The argument put forward by Sylos-Labini was that *"the proportional margin* [that is, the mark-up] *tends to decrease when direct costs increase and it tends to increase when these costs decrease"*[3]. To explain his point the author drew on considerations about the role of demand for the firm and for the potential entry of new firms in oligopolistic markets. In particular, in the presence of an increase in "*direct costs*" due to money-wages growing faster than productivity, firms prefer not to transfer completely that increase onto prices, with a view to encouraging the expansion of demand and, at the same time, avoiding the entry of new firms in that market. An increase in prices which is less than proportional with respect to the increase in "direct costs" implies a reduction in the "proportional margin".

Similarly, in the case of a reduction in "*direct costs*" the decrease in prices is less than proportional, expecially if foreign competition is not a binding constraint and the increase in average productivity is due to the introduction of innovations not accessible to all firms. Then, the result is an increase in the "proportional margin".

---

3 P. Sylos-Labini (1967), p. 277. See also the comment in Chapter II, note 20 of the present work.

These arguments confirm the relevance of demand and capacity utilisation in the decisions of the firms in imperfectly competitive markets. In fact, as is well known, within perfectly competitive settings firms face an infinitely elastic demand for their output, whereas if competition is not perfect they have to engage in pricing strategies, taking account of the effects on their own market-share and, consequently, on the utilisation of their productive capacity. It should be noticed, by the way, that Kalecki (1954) had already made this point, when explaining the mark-up and the degree of monopoly power of firms.

The above formulation of the price changes, and therefore, of firms' margins, makes it possible to take account of the behaviour of firms' costs without neglecting the importance of demand, by letting the latter explain the elasticity of price variations with respect to costs variations, in a given economy.

The role of demand may be further enhanced by introducing an additional component of price changes which takes into account the presence of a "direct" effect of the demand pressure on prices. This can be signalled by the behaviour of real liquidity, which is supposed to act as an indicator of the "state of demand", in particular of the demand equipped with purchasing power. The idea is that the availability of liquidity (in real terms) "finances" expenditure, whereas the shortage of purchasing power discourages it. Consequently, firms' pricing strategies will be oriented towards re-establishing profit margins in periods of abundant liquidity and high spending, and vice-versa in periods of scarce liquidity and low spending.

By taking into consideration both determinants, the growth rate of prices is here specified in the following terms:

$$\dot{p}/p = (\frac{\xi}{1+\xi})\left[\frac{\dot{w}}{w} - \frac{\dot{x}}{x}\right] + b(H - \overline{H}), \qquad \xi > 0,\ b > 0 \qquad [3.8']$$

where $\xi/(1+\xi) < 1$, for the above points regarding the cost-price dynamics in imperfectly competitive markets, $H \equiv M / pK$ is the overall liquidity in real terms and $\overline{H}$ is the "normal" or "average" level of H.

The equation above implies[4] that the law of motion for firms' mark-up m is:

$$\frac{\dot{m}}{m} = -(\frac{1}{1+\xi})\left[\frac{\dot{w}}{w} - \frac{\dot{x}}{x}\right] + b(H - \overline{H}). \qquad [3.8]$$

As for the productivity of labour $x = X/N$, it is assumed that it moves according to the following law:

$$x(t) = X(t)/ N(t) = x(t_0)e^{\lambda(t-t_0)}$$

where λ is the proportionate rate of growth of the labour productivity. Then, in terms of rates of changes we have:

$$\dot{x} / x = \lambda. \qquad [3.9]$$

As to the "state of confidence" of firms, which is measured by the behaviour of variable ρ, several factors govern its motion over time. It has already been mentioned that, within the context of imperfectly competitive markets, demand plays a crucial role in firms' decision-making, since each firm is highly concerned about a possible threat to its own market-share. Leaving

4 To show this, note that the logarithmic differentiation of equation [3.4] with respect to time yields: $\dot{p} / p = \dot{m} / m + \dot{w} / w - \dot{x} / x$. Hence, equation [3.8'] implies that the law of motion that governs the mark-up m is given by equation [3.8].

aside, for the sake of simplicity, other factors which affect the "state of confidence", it is assumed here that the degree of capacity utilisation constitutes the indicator of the performance of future demand, and the factor that governs the motion of ρ. Therefore, the "state of confidence" of firms is governed by:

$$\dot{\rho} = \alpha\,[\frac{X}{K}], \qquad [3.10]$$

where $\alpha[..]$ is a positive function[5].

It is then assumed that the expected rate of price inflation π^e obeys an adjustment scheme of the "adaptive" type, given by the differential equation:

$$\dot{\pi}^e = \beta\,(\frac{\dot{p}}{p} - \pi^e), \qquad \beta > 0 \qquad [3.11]$$

the solution of which is:

$$\pi^e(t) = \pi^e(t_o)e^{-\beta(t-t_0)} + \beta \int_{t_0}^{t} e^{-\beta\,(t-s)}\pi(s)\,ds$$

so that[6] $\pi^e(t)$ is formed as a geometric "distributed lag" of past actual rates of inflation $\pi \equiv \dot{p}/p$.

To complete the model, the laws of motion of *M* and *K* are specified. As a first approximation, it is assumed that the supply of money grows uniformly at a given exogenous rate μ:

---

5 Later in the course of this Chapter some variants for the function will be considered.

6 This can be verified by applying " Leibnitz's rule". Cf. T. J. Sargent (1987), Chapter V: "Dynamic Analysis of a Keynesian Model".

$$\dot{M} / M = \mu . \qquad [3.12]$$

As to the stock of capital K, it is formed through the flow of net investment which, assuming no depreciation, coincides with gross investment. The associated equation is:

$$I / K = \dot{K} / K$$

which provides the specification of equation [3.2].

Consequently, the time path of the stock of capital is given by:

$$K(t) = K(t_0) + \int_{t_0}^{t} [I / K](s) K(s) ds .$$

The model is completed by adding the law of motion for the supply of labour N^S, which is the variable showing in equation [3.7]. The assumption common to most growth models and adopted here is that the supply of labour grows at a constant and exogenous rate n, that is:

$$\dot{N}^S / N^S = n ,$$

and so the labour supply is governed by:

$$N^S(t) = N^S(t_0) e^{n(t-t_0)} . \qquad [3.13]$$

Putting all equations together, the resulting model is made of the following thirteen equations:

$$C/K = (w/p)N/K + c_\pi [(X - (w/p)N]/K \qquad 0 < c_\pi < 1 \qquad [3.1]$$

$$I/K = \dot{K}/K = \gamma[((X - (w/p)N)/K + \rho) - (i - \pi^e)] \qquad \gamma' > 0 \qquad [3.2]$$

$$N/K = (1/x)\, X/K \qquad [3.3]$$

$$p = m\,(w/x) \qquad m > 1 \qquad [3.4]$$

$$X/K = C/K + \dot{K}/K \qquad [3.5]$$

$$M/pK = h\,(X/K, i) \qquad h_y' > 0;\ h_i' < 0 \qquad [3.6]$$

$$\dot{w}/w = f(N/N^S) + \dot{\pi}^e \qquad f' > 0 \qquad [3.7]$$

$$\frac{\dot{m}}{m} = -(\frac{1}{1+\xi})\left[\frac{\dot{w}}{w} - \frac{\dot{x}}{x}\right] + b(H - \overline{H}) \qquad \xi > 0;\ b > 0 \qquad [3.8]$$

$$\dot{x}/x = \lambda \qquad [3.9]$$

$$\dot{\rho} = \alpha\,[\frac{X}{K}] \qquad \alpha' > 0 \qquad [3.10]$$

$$\dot{\pi}^e = \beta\,(\frac{\dot{p}}{p} - \pi^e) \qquad \beta > 0 \qquad [3.11]$$

$$\frac{\dot{H}}{H} = \mu - \frac{\dot{p}}{p} - \dot{K}/K \qquad [3.12]$$

$$\dot{N}^S/N^S = n \qquad [3.13]$$

where, as stated above: $H \equiv M/pK$.

Given the initial conditions for each differential equation, the model generates time paths of the thirteen endogenous variables: $X/K, N/K, C/K, K, M, i, p, m, w, \rho, x, \pi^e, N^S$.

As explained in Section 3.2, the first six equations may be reduced to two equations, the IS and the LM curves, which give the short-run equilibrium of the model. This may, in general, be a non-stationary equilibrium, and the system would then be characterised by income distribution, the output-capital ratio, that is, the degree of capacity utilisation, and the rate of interest changing over time.

In a *steady-state* situation these quantities are at the constant equilibrium level, and the system moves at the "natural rate", $(n + \lambda)$, that is, the sum of the growth rates of the labour force and productivity. Moreover, in a steady state real wages grow at a rate equal to the growth rate of productivity, and the supply of money at a rate equal to the sum of the growth rates of prices and the capital stock – the latter being equal to $(n + \lambda)$, in a steady state.

Formally, since in a steady-state position the output-capital ratio and the interest rate are constant, that is, $[X/K = (X/K)^*]$ and $[i = i^*]$, the money demand function in real terms $h(X/K, i)$ is constant, too. From equation [3.6] it then follows that $H \equiv M / pK$ should be constant, too.

Hence, from equation [3.12] it results:

$$\dot{M}/M - \dot{p}/p - \dot{K}/K = 0. \qquad [3.12^*]$$

Taking account of the fact that in a steady state:

$$\dot{K}/K = (n + \lambda),$$

after substituting it into [3.12*] the following condition is obtained:

$$\mu - \dot{p}/p - (n + \lambda) = 0.$$

It is interesting to analyse the mechanisms that govern the dynamic behaviour of the model through a diagrammatic representation of the system.

In the [(X/K)-i] plane the IS and the LM curves are plotted for the "temporary" or short-run equilibrium. Two more curves are plotted to characterise the steady-state path[7].

The first is a vertical line at the steady-state output-capital ratio $(X/K)^*$, that is, the output-capital ratio at which the accumulation rate is "consistent" with the natural rate of growth $(n + \lambda)$.

To obtain the value of $(X/K)^*$, consider that in a steady state the following relationship holds:

$$\dot{X} / X = \dot{K} / K = (n + \lambda).$$

Hence, the (dynamic) equilibrium between the flows of savings and investment, per unit of capital, is given by the condition:

$$S/K = n + \lambda$$

and, finally, the following result is obtained:

$$\frac{X}{K} - \frac{C}{K} - (n + \lambda) = 0$$

$$\frac{X}{K} - (\frac{W}{X})\frac{X}{K} - c_\pi (1 - \frac{W}{X})\frac{X}{K} - (n + \lambda) = 0$$

$$\frac{X}{K} - c_\pi \frac{X}{K} - (1 - c_\pi)\frac{W}{X}\frac{X}{K} - (n + \lambda) = 0$$

$$s\frac{X}{K} - s\frac{W}{X}\frac{X}{K} - (n + \lambda) = 0$$

7 Cf. T. J. Sargent (1987), Ch. V: "Dynamic Analysis of a Keynesian Model".

$$s\frac{X}{K}(1-\frac{1}{m})-(n+\lambda)=0\,,$$

which yield the steady-state equilibrium value:

$$(\frac{X}{K})^{*}=\frac{n+\lambda}{s(1-1/m)}\,. \qquad [I]$$

The steady-state value $(X/K)^*$ is independent of the rate of interest, whereas it is influenced by the value of m, that is by income distribution. Hence, in the $[(X/K)\text{-}i]$ plane a steady-state vertical line is plotted at $(X/K)^*$, the position of which depends on the value of m.

The second curve, denoted by KK, is obtained by setting the condition that the desired accumulation of firms, according to the function $\gamma\,[\ldots]$, is consistent with the steady-state growth rate $(n + \lambda)$, that is:

$$\gamma[\frac{X}{K}(1-\frac{1}{m})+\rho-(i-\pi^{e})]-(n+\lambda)=0\,. \qquad [II]$$

This equation gives the set of all points $\{(X/K); (i - \pi^e)\}$ at which the system is in a dynamic equilibrium, given m and hence income distribution and given ρ. Therefore, it indicates what the value of the real rate of interest $(i - \pi^e)$ is at a given output-capital ratio (X/K), for the system to be in equilibrium over time.

By totally differentiating equation [II], the following expression for the slope of the KK curve is obtained:

$$\frac{d(i-\pi^{e})}{d(X/K)}=(1-\frac{1}{m})$$

which is positive and equal to the profit-share.

The IS and KK curves intersect at the steady-state value $(X/K)^*$, as can be verified after the substitution of equation [II] into the IS equation:

$$\frac{X}{K} = \frac{C}{K} + (n + \lambda)$$

from which equation [I] is once again obtained:

$$(\frac{X}{K})^* = \frac{n + \lambda}{s(1 - 1/m)}.$$

The vertical line passing through $(X/K)^*$ together with the KK curve are plotted in the diagram of Figure [3.1].

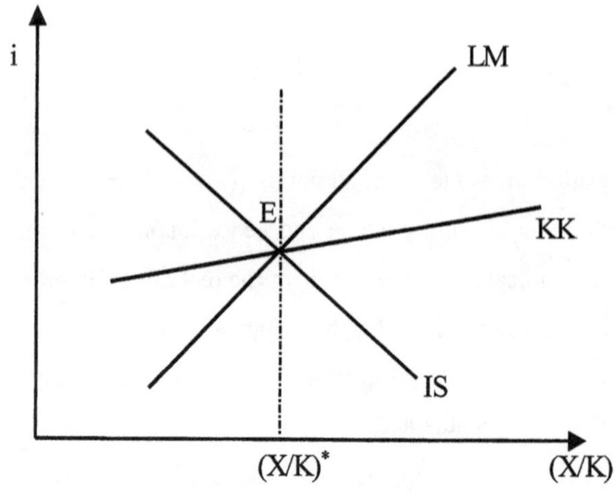

Figure 3.1. *The steady-state equilibrium in model I*

The IS and the KK curves intersect at point *E*, where $(X/K) = (X/K)^*$. In the case represented in the diagram[8], the short-run equilibrium, which is located at the IS-LM intersection, is also at point *E*.

The following interpretation of the diagram can be given. The IS, LM and KK curves are plotted for given values of the exogenous variables, at a point in time. The curves shift following "jumps" (i.e. once-and-for-all changes) in the exogenous variables, as in Figure (3.2).

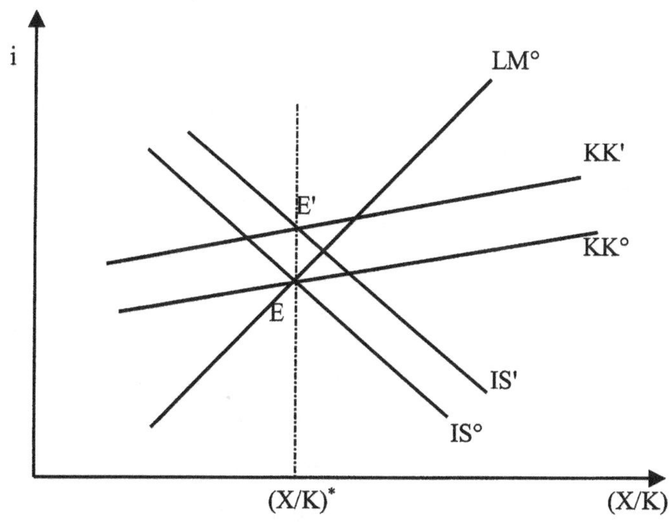

Figure 3.2. *The effect of once-and-for-all jumps in* ρ *and* π^e *on the IS and KK curves*

In particular, the KK° shifts upwards following a (positive) jump in ρ or in π^e. In fact, with the accumulation proceeding at the rate $(n + \lambda)$, a higher rate of

8 In the analysis that follows a downward sloping IS curve is implicitly assumed, that is $(s - \gamma') > 0$.

interest is required at each level of (X/K), *coeteris paribus*, for the system to be in equilibrium over time.

Moreover, the IS° curve shifts upwards, following the aforesaid jumps. It is evident from the diagram that point *E'*, that is the new intersection point of the IS' and KK' curves, is still at $X/K = (X/K)^*$.

A once-and-for-all (positive) jump in *m*, the firms' "proportional margin", which leads to an increase in the profit-share, has a positive effect on the desired level of accumulation and a negative impact on aggregate consumption. This causes an upward shift of the KK curve and a leftward shift of the intersection point of the IS and the LM curves. The latter effect is due to the fact that, with a downward sloping IS, the overall impact of an increase in the profit-share on the equilibrium level of income is negative[9].

As to the LM curve, it moves to the right in the case of a once-and-for-all (positive) jump in *M*.

The dynamic behaviour of the model may be sketched out by referring once more to the curves plotted in Figure (3.1). Consider the initial situation in which the IS-LM equilibrium is given at the steady-state value $(X/K)^*$. A steady-state "full equilibrium" is said to be achieved with an unchanging distribution of income through time, and if real wages grow at the growth rate of productivity. In this case, the IS, LM and KK curves do not shift over time. Equation [3.7] gives the equilibrium rate of employment: $E = (N/N^S) = (N/N^S)^*$.

In order to understand the mechanisms that govern the dynamics of the model, consider the behaviour of the system off the steady-state equilibrium, according to equations [3.1] – [3.13] of the model.

First of all, every time the IS and LM curves intersect at an $(X/K,\ i)$ combination which is below the KK curve, accumulation is proceeding faster

9 Cf. Appendix B.1.

than the steady-state rate $(n + \lambda)$. This happens because the rate of interest i is lower than the one required for the system to be in equilibrium, at that level of the output-capital ratio (X/K). If, instead, the intersection point is above the KK curve, capital is decreasing more slowly than the steady-state rate $(n + \lambda)$.

Suppose that the IS-LM equilibrium is at the $(X/K, i)$ combination located at point A, as in the diagram in Figure (3.3), whereas the steady-state combination $[(X/K)^*, i^*]$ is at point E, at the intersection of the IS and KK curves. To simplify the analysis, assume for the moment that π^e is at its equilibrium level, unchanging through time.

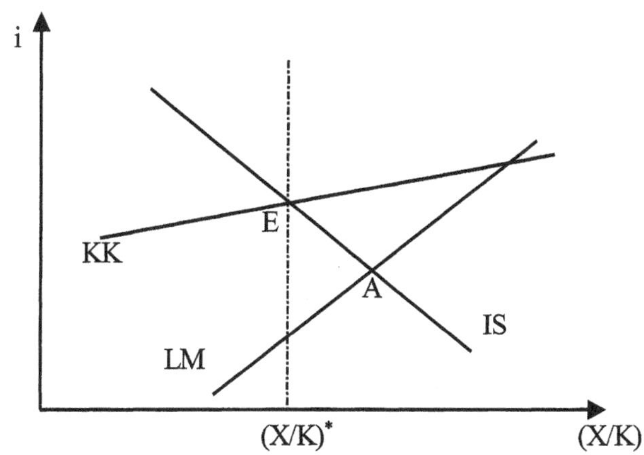

Figure 3.3. *The short-run equilibrium and the steady-state position*

The IS and LM curves intersect at point A, below the KK curve, where $(X/K) > (X/K)^*$ and $i < i^*$. Firms' reaction is to increase the stock of capital at a rate greater than the steady-state rate of point E, according to the investment function $\gamma[\ldots]$. Hence, at point A the following condition holds:

$$\dot{K}/K-(n+\lambda)>0.$$

Moreover, at point *A* the rate of employment is greater than the equilibrium rate, which is at point *E*, so that money wages are growing faster than the equilibrium rate, according to equation [3.7]. The same is true for prices, which move on the basis of equation [3.8']. Since real wages are growing faster than productivity, firms' margins are decreasing over time, that is:

$$\dot{w}/w-\dot{p}/p-\lambda>0.$$

Therefore, the growth rate of price inflation is positive $[(\dot{p}/p)>0]$, but less than the growth rate of "direct costs" $[\dot{w}/w-\lambda]$, and margins are decreasing over time $[(\dot{m}/m)<0]$, so that the wage-share is increasing. This result occurs if in equation [3.8'] the cost-side determinant of price changes, through coefficient $\xi/(1+\xi)$, prevails over the component which is related to the (direct) demand effect, via[10] coefficient *b*.

As long as the stock of capital keeps growing faster than the steady-state rate and the growth rate of price inflation is greater than the equilibrium rate, condition [3.12*]:

$$\dot{M}/M-\dot{p}/p-\dot{K}/K=0$$

is not satisfied, and the LM curve shifts upwards over time. This can be verified by considering the logarithmic differentiation with respect to time of the LM

10 The specific role of the two determinants, which ultimately affect the changes in the distribution of income, will be examined in more detail later in this Chapter, in the course of the analysis of the dynamics of the model.

curve - equation [3.6] – for a fixed value of (*X/K*), and then by solving it for the rate of interest *i*:

$$\dot{i}\Big|_{LM} = \frac{h[(X/K),i]}{h_i^{'}}\left[\frac{\dot{M}}{M} - \frac{\dot{p}}{p} - \frac{\dot{K}}{K}\right], \qquad \text{[A]}$$

which says that, if the expression in brackets is negative, then the LM equilibrium condition requires increasing values of the interest rate *i* over time.

At point *A*, since $(X/K) > (X/K)^*$, firms have positive expectations on the evolution of aggregate demand, which leads to an improvement in the state of confidence, according to equation [3.10].

This drives the IS and the KK curves upwards over time. In fact, rewriting the IS curve in the form:

$$\frac{X}{K} = \frac{W}{X}\frac{X}{K} + c_\pi(1-\frac{W}{X})\frac{X}{K} + \gamma\left[(1-\frac{W}{X})\frac{X}{K} + \rho - (i-\pi^e)\right] \qquad \text{[3.5^]}$$

which can be expressed, equivalently, in the following terms:

$$S/K - \dot{K}/K = s(1-\frac{1}{m})\frac{X}{K} - \gamma\left[(1-\frac{1}{m})\frac{X}{K} + \rho - (i-\pi^e)\right] = 0 \qquad \text{[3.5*]}$$

then, the logarithmic differentiation with respect to time of equation [3.5*], for given values of *X/K*, and by solving it for *i*, yields:

$$\dot{i}\Big|_{IS} = \left[\frac{\gamma[..]}{\gamma'}\right]\left[\left(s - \frac{\gamma'}{\gamma[..]}\right)\left(\frac{X}{K}\right)\right]\left[-\frac{\dot{m}}{m}\right] + \frac{\dot{\rho}}{\rho}. \qquad \text{[B]}$$

Condition [B] states that increasing values of ρ over time require increasing values of the interest rate i to keep equilibrium in the goods markets – *coeteris paribus*.

Similarly, for the KK curve: the logarithmic differentiation with respect to time of equation [II], and by solving it for the rate of interest, yields:

$$\dot{i}\Big|_{KK} = (\frac{X}{K})\frac{\dot{m}}{m} + \frac{\dot{\rho}}{\rho}. \qquad [C]$$

The two expressions [B] and [C] above show that changes in income distribution affect the position of the IS and the LM curves, too. In particular, decreasing values of m cause the IS curve to move upwards over time - if the terms in brackets (s - γ'/γ) is positive, that is, if the IS curve is downward sloping - and the KK curve to move downwards.

Altogether, therefore, the IS curve shifts upwards, whereas the movement of the KK curve depends on the relative size of (the contrasting effects of) the improvement in the state of confidence and of the decrease in the margins.

The shift of the three curves over time, which determines the trajectory of the system starting from point A, is illustrated in the diagram in Figure (3.4), where it is assumed that the KK curve shifts upwards.

As indicated by the arrows, the IS and the LM curves move towards an intersection which is still below the KK curve, as for instance the one corresponding to point A_1; hence, the adjustment process is not yet complete, and the shift of the three curves continues.

When enough time has passed for the shifts of the IS, LM and KK curves to take place, the three curves intersect again. This situation is illustrated in the graph in Figure (3.5), where the intersection point of the three curves is denoted as A_2.

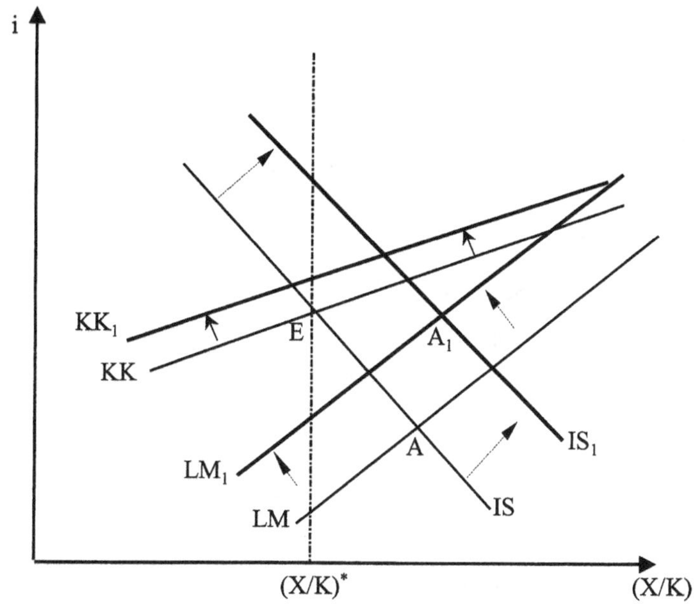

Figure 3.4. *Shifts of the IS, LM and KK curves out of the steady state*

Yet, at this stage the adjustment process is not complete, since during all the intervening period the stock of capital has grown faster than the steady-state rate $(n + \lambda)$, so that at A_2 the rate of employment $E = (1/x)(X/N)(K/N^S)$ exceeds its equilibrium level, and thus money wages are growing faster than productivity.

With income distribution still changing over time the system is not yet at a "full" steady-state equilibrium and the LM curve keeps shifting upwards over time. In the course of the adjustment process, the LM curve moves to subsequent intersections with the IS curve above the KK curve (as at point A_3), so that the system "overshoots", with $(X/K) < (X/K)^*$ and $i > i^*$, and with the accumulation rate below the steady-state rate, that is:

$\dot{K}/K < (n+\lambda)$.

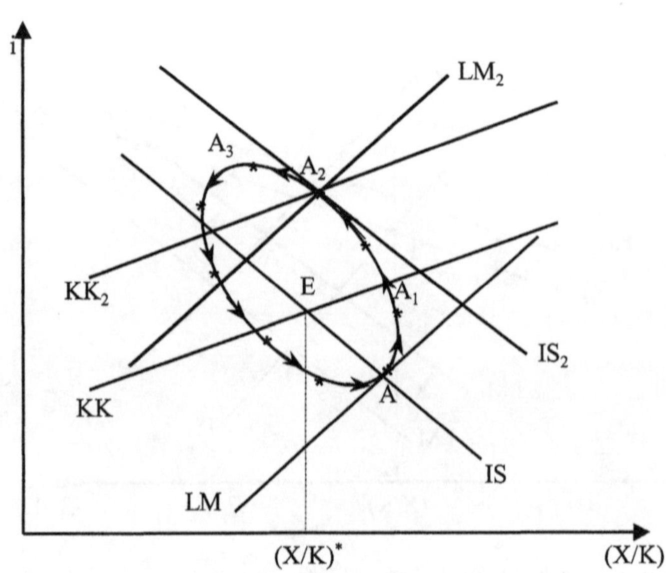

Figure 3.5. *The trajectory of the system*

Money wages keep rising above the equilibrium rate, and thus prices are growing too, although at successive lower rates. Hence, the LM curve keeps moving upwards.

As for the IS and KK curves, the upwards shift over time proceeds until the output-capital ratio exceeds its equilibrium level, leading to an improvement in the state of confidence and a shift in income distribution in favour of the wage-share. The movement is reversed when, given stability, the effect of negative expectations on the rate of capacity utilisation, which feeds back to the desired accumulation of firms, dominates, thus shifting the IS and the KK curves downwards towards their initial positions.

And given stability, the direction of the movement of the LM curve is reversed when the (stabilising) effect of a decreasing accumulation dominates the (de-stabilising) effect of the wage-price dynamics, thus yielding:

$$\dot{M}/M - \dot{p}/p - \dot{K}/K < 0.$$

Once N/N^S has fallen below its equilibrium level, as a consequence of the decrease in accumulation, the growth rate of money wages also falls below the steady-state equilibrium rate, and the LM curve moves towards the right.

It is possible that once the system has reached the equilibrium position again and the three curves intersect, a new overshooting occurs towards another "boom" period, with money wages increasing over time.

Altogether, the trajectory of the system could be an oscillatory one, with alternating periods of boom and recession.

The consideration of anticipated inflation π^e has the effect of accentuating the cyclical phenomenon. In fact, an increase in π^e over time shifts the IS and KK curves upwards, and the two curves continue to intersect at $(X/K)^*$, *coeteris paribus*[11].

As for the variable ρ, earlier in the Chapter the law of motion of ρ (equation [3.10]) was given in an implicit form:

$$\dot{\rho} = \alpha\,[X/K]$$

with α left as a positive unspecified function. Of course, different assumptions can be made on the specific form of the function, and clearly a different *scenario* will emerge with the specification adopted in particular.

11 For a similar argument, see T. J. Sargent (1987), Chapter V.

For instance, assume the following explicit formulation of equation [3.10]:

$$\dot{\rho} = v_0 + v_1 y - v_2 y^2, \quad v_0 < 0, v_1 > 0, v_2 \geq 0.$$

where $y \equiv X / K$. If the second-order term coefficient v_2 is positive, then the function describing the motion of the firms' "state of confidence" is non-linear with respect to y; by setting $v_2 = 0$, instead, the function becomes linear.

The above formulation takes account of two different factors. First of all, the increase in demand and in the rate of capacity utilisation constitutes an important signal which affects positively the "state of confidence" of firms, that is, the expectations of investment profitability over time. This is particularly true within the context of imperfectly competitive markets. Secondly, firms may fear the negative effect of an expanding demand on the behaviour of costs over time, and consequently on the performance of profit margins during the cycle. This factor would then explain the second-order term[12].

The diagram of Figure (3.6) illustrates two non-linear functions, each corresponding to different values of coefficients v_1 and v_2.

Curve *a* refers to firms which are relatively more optimistic in following the expansion of demand when updating their expectations. In this case, the decreasing segment of the curve is not so steep and the function changes sign at the higher values of y. Curve *b*, instead, shows the case of firms whose "state of confidence" moves relatively more cautiously with the expansion of demand.

---

12 In reality, it may happen that concern about the effects of the dynamics of costs on the margins is reflected itself in changes in technology in the long-run, thus affecting the accumulation process. A broader model would be required to deal with this issue. Because of its importance in the accumulation decisions in the actual working of markets, it should be considered in further extensions of the analysis.

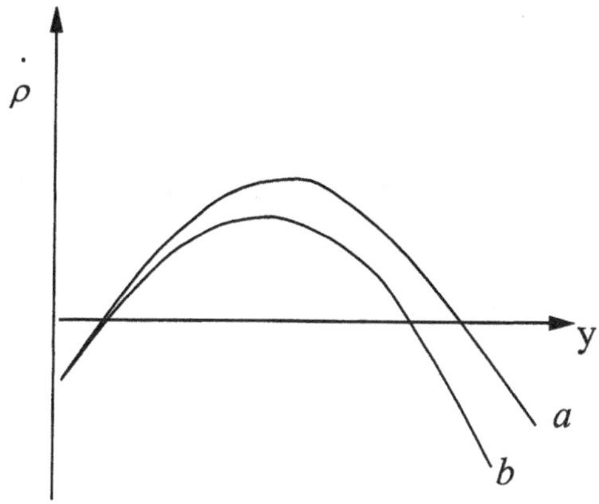

Figure 3.6. *Different shapes of the "state of confidence" function*

The consideration into the analysis of the "state of confidence" could make the model more susceptible to instability. In terms of the diagrammatic framework employed, the change in ρ affects the shift of the IS and KK curves over time[13], thus accentuating the amplitude of fluctuations. In particular, other things being equal, the system tends to lose stability the higher the sensitivity of the state of confidence to the rate of capacity utilisation y, and so, for instance more easily in the case of curve *a* rather than curve *b* (Fig. 3.6).

The analysis makes it possible to draw some conclusions about the difference between the characteristics of the model which has been presented in this Chapter and the models in the literature surveyed in Chapter II.

First of all, models building on the basic Goodwin framework (1967) emphasize the existence of a cycle in the rate of employment and the wage-share. Here, in addition to the aforementioned dynamic interaction, the rate of

13 Cf. equations [B] and [C] in this Chapter.

capacity utilisation is allowed to vary over the cycle, instead of being assumed fixed at the full utilisation level. Accordingly, the short-run equilibrium, which is determined at the intersection of the IS and LM curves, may well be achieved at a level of aggregate demand, and its associated capacity utilisation rate, which is different from the "normal" or "average" level, corresponding to the long-run or steady-state equilibrium level.

Therefore, this analysis makes it possible to account for an important "stylised fact" of business cycles, that is, the fluctuation of aggregate demand and of the capacity utilisation rate, which, instead, was left aside in that literature.

Moreover, the importance of demand is confirmed and enhanced by its influence on firms' pricing strategies and its role on the "state of confidence", which affects investment decisions.

All this explains why an increase in the wage-share does not lead immediately to a reduction in investment, as in the typical "Classical" theoretical perspective and in the Goodwin model, since investment decisions are affected by the behaviour of aggregate demand, too, and not only by the profit-share of the firms.

Moreover, in comparison with a "traditional" dynamic Keynesian model[14] with an aggregate consumption function and prices determined on the basis of the marginal productivity, the cyclical dynamics of the model presented here is more complex.

There, in fact, the effects of changes in income distribution are not at issue, and thus the shift over time of the LM curve takes place along an IS curve which

---

14 An example of the "standard" Keynesian dynamic modelling (in the sense of the "Neo-classical synthesis), can be found in T. J. Sargent (1987), Ch. V, in which the graph of Figure (3.6) is illustrated.

does not move over time, like the KK curve[15], as in the case illustrated in Figure (3.7).

The system would then move along a trajectory from point *A* to point *Z* and again, in the opposite direction, towards point *A*.

The analysis developed up to this point illustrates the dynamic behaviour of the model, sketching the mechanisms that govern the motion of the relevant variables over time and giving a diagrammatic interpretation of the behaviour of the system out of the steady-state equilibrium position.

Analytical details of the stability issues are developed in Appendix B, whilst the main features and results are briefly outlined in what follows.

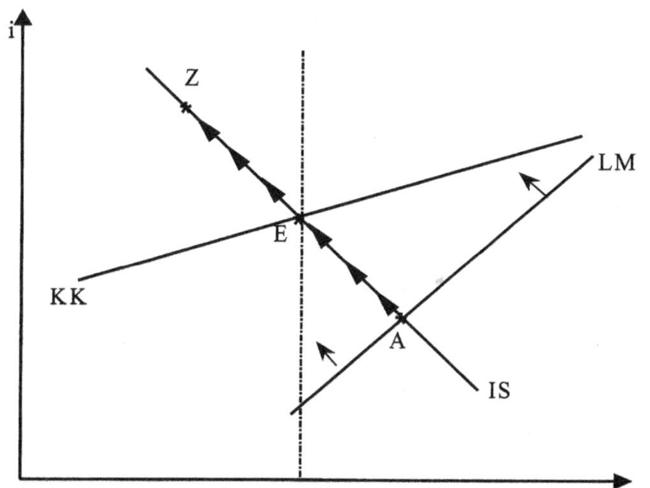

Figure 3.7. *The trajectory in a "standard" Keynesian dynamic model*

15 This, of course, leaving aside the effects of ρ and π^e. On this point, cf. T. J. Sargent (1987), Ch. V.

The analysis has been accomplished by reducing the "size" of the system and simplifying the model through the omission of the two variables ρ, the "state of confidence", and π^e, the expected inflation. Their role will be reconsidered in the second step of the analysis. The following simpler system is thus obtained:

$$\begin{aligned} \dot{m}/m &= -a[f(E)-\lambda]+b(H-\overline{H}) \\ \dot{E}/E &= \dot{y}/y+g(m,H)-(n+\lambda) \\ \dot{H}/H &= \mu-\dot{p}/p-g(m,H) \end{aligned} \qquad [S1]$$

where $y \equiv X/K$, $a \equiv \xi/(1+\xi)$ and $g(m,H) \equiv \dot{K}/K$.

From the short-run equilibrium solution of the IS-LM model it is possible to obtain[16] the expression for $\dot{y}/y$, and by taking into account equation [3.8'] for the rate of price inflation $\dot{p}/p$, system [S1] may be expressed[17] in terms of the three variables: *m*, *E* and *H*.

By approximating linearly around the equilibrium point (or points) of system [S1], it is possible to have information on the "local" behaviour of the system. For this purpose, the preliminary step is to calculate the stationary solution corresponding to the long-run equilibrium of the model. Then, to evaluate the *Jacobian*. On these bases, the following Routh-Hurwicz stability conditions are given:

(*i*) $a_2 = (-\mathrm{tr}\,J) > 0$;
(*ii*) $a_1 = (\Sigma\,\text{principal minors of } J) > 0$;

16 Cf. Appendix B.1.
17 Cf. Appendix B.2.

(*iii*) $a_0 = (-\det J) > 0$;

(*iv*) $a_1 a_2 - a_0 > 0$.

These conditions guarantee that the roots of the characteristic polynomial, $\lambda^3 + a_2\lambda^2 + a_1\lambda + a_0 = 0$, have all negative real part[18].

In general, the nature of the equilibrium point and the dynamic behaviour of the model depend on the parameters appearing in the system, since they affect both the equilibrium solution and the *Jacobian*, thus determining the sign of the conditions (*i*)-(*iv*). As one or more parameters change, the system may undergo a qualitative variation in the nature of the singular points and of the trajectories: this variation may be the source of a *bifurcation*, a term indicating the situation in which a system, which initially is in a stable equilibrium, loses its stability as the parameter changes, at a "critical" value also known as the *bifurcation* value, thus giving rise to closed orbits[19].

In the present model parameter a is a possible source of bifurcation. As it results from a numerical illustration in Appendix B, for relative small values of a the system has stable solutions, whereas if the value of a increases there is a change in the nature of the solutions[20].

---

18 In particular, in the case in which the relations (*i*)-(*iii*) are all satisfied, whereas relation (*iv*) is not, the system admits at least one pair of imaginary roots, i.e. there are periodic solutions, if $a_1a_2 - a_0 = 0$; it has, instead, one root with negative real part and two roots with positive real part if $a_1a_2 - a_0 < 0$ is obtained and, hence, the system is unstable.

19 This is the case, for instance, of the *Hopf* bifurcations. In Appendix B.2 the *Hopf* Theorem is given, with the *sufficient* conditions for the *existence* of closed orbits.

20 Cf. Appendix B.3. In particular, while still within the range of values at which the system is stable, some negative *real* roots become *complex* with negative real part. At the critical value of a where condition (*iv*) is not satisfied any longer and $a_1a_2 - a_0 = 0$, the *Jacobian* has a negative real root and two pure imaginary roots. Therefore, the system loses stability and periodic solutions emerge. Then, once above the critical value of a, not all the conditions (*i*)-(*iv*) are satisfied anymore and the system becomes unstable. Cf. the numerical illustration in Appendix B.3.

The economic interpretation of the role of parameter a in the dynamics of the model is the following. From the equation of the growth rate of prices:

$$\frac{\dot{p}}{p} = (1-a)\left[\frac{\dot{w}}{w} - \frac{\dot{x}}{x}\right] + b(H - \overline{H})$$

it results that (1 - a) measures the degree of the shift onto prices of the variation in "direct costs" through time. Within the context of imperfectly competitive markets, there may be, at the aggregate level, a certain "*inertia*" in the behaviour of prices with respect to the changes in "direct costs", because of the importance a firm gives to a sufficiently stable market-share and its fear of competitors' reactions. This affects the changes in income distribution over time: in the expansionary stage of the cycle, the profit-share decreases, while the capacity utilization increases. And vice-versa, in the contractionary phases the profit-share increases and correspondingly the rate of capacity utilization decreases[21].

The result of this analysis is that parameters a and b may be a source of instability. In particular, as parameter a is increased the system might lose stability, and vice-versa for parameter b, which acts in the opposite direction[22]. Parameter b in both equations of the growth rates of the margin and of prices has an effect which is the opposite (in sign) of parameter a's effect.

The economic interpretation of all this is that the further away the market structure is from a perfectly competitive setting, the more the behaviour of firms towards pricing strategies is conditioned by the behaviour of potential competitors and the uncertainty of demand, and therefore the higher the degree of *inertia* in the price adjustment to changes in costs, and thus the value of parameter a .

21 This point was made clear earlier in this Chapter. Cf. note 3 (this Chapter).
22 Cf. Appendix B.3.

The point may easily be seen in terms of the graphic analysis made earlier in the Chapter. With reference to Figure (3.8), when the system is off the steady state the IS, LM and KK curves shift over time. For values of parameter *a* above a certain critical value, the trajectory of the system may diverge. In fact, since this parameter determines the degree of the growth rate of the margin, the first equation of system [S1], and consequently of the growth rate of prices, it determines the specific trajectory of the system over time, that is the "relative" shift of the IS and LM curves.

The diagram illustrates the case in which starting from point *A*, the successive intersections of the IS and LM curves take place along the trajectory indicated as "*z*". In this case, the cost-price dynamics, and the consequent variations in income distribution in favour of the wage-share, transforms the "boom" into a "burst".

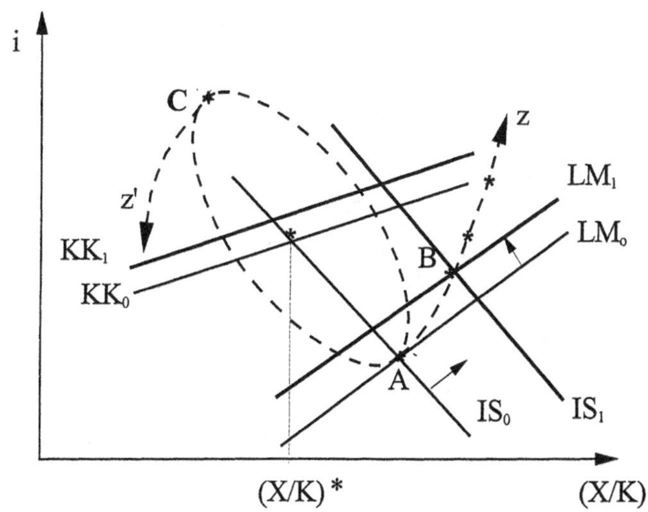

Figure 3.8. *The behaviour of the system off the steady state, in the case of diverging trajectories*

On the other hand, if the system is at point C, then the impact of the cost-price dynamics on income distribution can cause a relevant downward shift in the IS curve over time, meanwhile the shift of the LM curve to the right is not so pronounced. Hence, the system moves along the trajectory denoted as "z'", and thus does not recover from the recession.

In short, one basic insight emerging from the model is the role of effective demand in the cyclical process. The full capacity utilisation is not always attained, and this is relevant in firms' pricing strategies and in the dynamics of income distribution. The latter, in turn, influences aggregate demand and the capacity utilisation rate. In this way, the "Classical" mechanism based on the feed back between changes in income-shares and in the employment rate is extended to aggregate demand and the capacity utilisation rate. This additional factor affects the features of the cyclical process and, as mentioned earlier, may be a source of instability. The higher parameter a is, the more pronounced the variations in income distribution in the cycle are and, consequently, the fluctuation of aggregate demand and of the associated capacity utilisation rate.

If the value of parameter a is one at which the system is unstable, a counter-cyclical monetary policy may succeed in "controlling" the dynamics of the model. Assume that the Central Bank expands the stock of money when the growth rate of income is below the average (or normal) rate and when the rate of employment is below the average rate, and vice-versa. The growth rate of the stock of money, in nominal terms, is thus expressible as the sum of a constant exogenous quantity μ and of a variable quantity ϕ in relation to the performance of the economy over the cycle. The latter may be expressed by a relation of the following type[23]:

---

23 A similar function is employed in Di Matteo (1984) to represent the counter-cyclical monetary policy rule. Here mark-up m takes the place of the wage-share, which was used in Di Matteo.

$$\phi = \delta \ (m - \overline{m}) - \theta \ (E - \overline{E}) \qquad [P.1]$$

where the above-average levels of margin *m* imply a below-average wage-share and, consequently, a growth rate of income below the average.

In particular, at given values of parameters *a* and *b*, there exists a range of values of the policy parameters δ and θ within which the system is stable, whereas with a fixed monetary policy rule (that is, with: $\delta = \theta = 0$) the system would be unstable[24].

24 Cf. Appendix B.4.

CHAPTER IV

Real and Financial Factors in Economic Fluctuations. An Extension of the Basic Model

4.1 – The Short-Run Equilibrium within an "Enlarged" IS-LM Framework

This Chapter extends the analysis by considering the role of financial factors in business fluctuations. In particular, it focuses on the role of the debt-financing of investment expenditure through the banking system, and the associated liquidity creation process, thus referring to a broader and endogenous concept of money.

As mentioned in the Introduction, the New Keynesian literature has placed emphasis on the factors determining the possibility that a "financing-hierarchy" exists from the point of view of the firm, which makes internal funds a preferred alternative to other forms of financing, whether credit or equity.

In many contributions of the literature which stress the role of the financial structure on investment decisions[1], it is assumed that firms are conditioned by the degree of their "self-financing" capacity, that is, their financial cash flow, on the basis of the principle that it reduces the bankruptcy risk.

This theoretical approach to the issue of the financing of investment draws, to some extent, on Kalecki's earlier intuitions (1937a) about the "principle of increasing risk"[2], according to which the rate of profit on reinvested profits

1 Cf. M. Gertler (1988); C. W. Calomiris – R. G. Hubbard (1990); B. Bernanke – M. Gertler (1987), (1990); D. Delli Gatti *et alii* (1993).

2 On this point, see also the comment in G. Vaciago (1987), pp. 121-125.

demanded by firms is lower than the rate of interest they would be willing to pay on financial liabilities, so that the latter incorporates a risk "premium".

Moreover, because of the possibility of *adverse selection* and *adverse incentive* problems, financial intermediaries resort to "non-price" *screening* mechanisms of borrowers by considering, for instance, the cash flow of firms not only as a "financial" indicator of their liquidity position, but also as an "economic" indicator of the expected future return of investment projects, and thus of the (bankruptcy) risk of the borrower.

In light of the theoretical micro-economic developments in the analysis of the working of credit markets in the presence of information problems, one may assume that the cash flow constitutes the way firms "signal" to the market the expected future return of their investment projects, that is, their "quality". Hence, the performance of cash flows might have a significant effect on the conditions of access to credit.

The monetary side of the model is modified with respect to the basic model I in order to take account of the fact that firms resort to bank credit to cover their financing needs. The latter is the "financing-gap", that is, the difference between the programmed expenditure and the internal funds, as defined by the firm's budget constraint. To simplify the analysis, and, at the same time, to emphasize the role of credit, other forms of financing are neglected.

The liquidity which is made available by the banking system through the credit process, that is, the "inside" money, has to be included in the definition of money together with the "outside" money, which is directly controlled by the monetary authorities. So, remembering the equilibrium condition for the money market given in equation [3.6']:

$$M^S = M^D \qquad [3.6']$$

the money supply M^S may, then, be expressed in the following way:

$$M^S = CC \qquad [a]$$

which says that the stock of money is equal to the volume of bank deposits *CC*, whilst notes and coins are not considered. The budget constraint of the banking sector is given by:

$$CC = R + LB + (D + F^S),$$

which shows that in front of a given amount of deposits *CC*, banks hold reserves to satisfy their liquidity demand, notably, the compulsory reserve *R* and the free reserves *LB*, held to face precautionary liquidity needs; and a volume of current debt, which may be expressed as the sum of the stock of accumulated (outstanding) debt *D* and the new flow of credit to firms, F^S.

Given the stock of existing debt *D*, the liquidity demand by the banking sector, in the form of compulsory and free reserves, represents a deduction from the credit circuit, given the constraint:

$$F^S + D = CC - R - LB.$$

Compliance with this constraint implies that, given *D*, the supply of finance F^S is equal to the difference between the amount of deposits *CC* and the compulsory and free reserves, *R* and *LB* respectively.

The analysis of the money supply according to the "standard" approach is generally made in terms of the market price mechanism. Yet, the risk associated with the non-fulfilment of the obligation on the side of the borrower means that the peculiarity of the working of credit markets must be accounted for according to the arguments put forward by the New Keynesian literature, as mentioned earlier. In fact, the borrowers' obligation is a *promise* of future payment, which is uncertain, whereas the bank credit outflow is a certain transaction. Therefore, the price alone – that is, the return expressed by the rate of interest – may not be a sufficient or adequate "signal" of the borrower's risk in the evaluation made by the bank as to the probability of *actually* obtaining the promised return.

In the present analysis, in order to emphasize the role of these factors in business cycles, it is assumed that the cash flow of firms is the relevant signal in banks' decisions as to the supply of credit, as suggested in the New Keynesian literature, leaving aside the traditional role of the rate of interest. In this way, the financial structure becomes relevant in the determination of the possibility for firms to realise the investment project.

Hence, leaving aside the free reserves *LB*, expression [a] may be reformulated in the following terms:

$$\begin{aligned} M^S &= R + D + F^S = R + D + \Phi(CF) = \\ &= R + D + \varphi[(X/K),\ (D/pK)], \qquad \varphi_1 > 0; \varphi_2 < 0 \end{aligned} \qquad [4.6a]$$

where the supply of finance F^S is a function of the firms' cash flow (*CF*), which is indicated here by income and the stock of real debt, both per unit of capital, that is, (X/K) and (D/pK), respectively.

As to the demand for money M^D, in the analysis of the basic model in Chapter III it was assumed to be related directly to income, by virtue of its being a means of payments in transactions, and inversely related to the rate of interest, as a measure of the opportunity cost of holding money instead of assets yielding a return equal to the market interest rate. Were money considered only as a means of payment, this inverse relation would be present in any case[3].

3 This result, as is well-known, stems from the so-called "square-root law" demonstrated by W. Baumol and J. Tobin in the "buffer stock approach" to the demand for money.

It is well known that Keynes, in a series of papers published in the *Economic Journal*[4] between 1937 and 1939, introduced a *finance motive* among the determinants of the demand for money. A wide debate and divergent interpretations still exist among economists on this *motive*. For instance, some authors explain it as the *increase* in the demand for money due to the increase in income and output[5]. According to Keynes, in fact, the existence of a *finance motive* for holding money has to do with the need for making production possible before demand has appeared in the market, and thus consistent with the principle that investment is independent of savings. Finance makes investment autonomous. It constitutes *"an advance provision of cash"*, *"...the credit required in the interval between planning and execution* [of expenditure]*"*. In Keynes's perspective, in the economic process *"liquidity disappears as finance while reappearing in the form of transactions* [and speculative] *balances"*[6].

To some extent, it seems very difficult to account for the *finance motive* for holding money (in this interpretation of Keynes's view) within an equilibrium analysis, just as when an IS-LM framework is employed. In this case, in fact, as has been pointed out[7], of the two cases only one is possible: either new liquidity has not yet been created, and money balances are still at the former level, or finance has been granted and the new liquidity, which is regularly used by firms

4 J. M. Keynes, "Alternative Theories of the Rate of Interest" (June 1937); "The ex-ante Theory of the Rate of Interest" (December 1937); "Comment on D. H. Robertson's 'Mr. Keynes' Finance" (1938); "The Process of Capital Formation" (1939).

5 This argument is generally made by many contemporary interpreters of Keynes's thought, among which are P. Davidson ["Keynes' Finance Motive", *Oxford Economic Papers*, 1965]. A very interesting critical analysis of the different points in the literature is made by A. Graziani (1984) according to whom "transactions balances" are financed by income, whereas "finance balances" are financed by debt. In this way, money turns out to be an endogenous variable.

6 Quoted from A. Graziani (1984).

7 Cf. A. Graziani (1984).

and eventually circulates in the economy as different types of incomes, generates transactions (and/or speculative) balances.

A possible way of including into the analysis the banking system within an IS-LM framework is to express the left side of equation [3.6'], that corresponds to the equilibrium condition for the money market, by using equation [4.6a] in which the liquidity creation process is made evident; the left side of equation [3.6'] would then be interpreted as the money balances with the new liquidity. This liquidity, which circulates in the economy in the form of the different types of incomes, generates a demand for "finance" balances, too, in addition to the transactions – and speculative – balances.

To sum up, then, the demand for money in the economy may be expressed[8] as the sum of a "traditional" component, i.e. the transactions and speculative balances, indicated by function $h(X, i)$, and an additional component for the "finance" motive F^D. Equation [3.6'] is hence reformulated in the following terms:

$$R + D + F^S = h(X, i) + F^D. \qquad [4.6^\wedge]$$

On the basis of the assumptions made, the finance demand is implicitly defined by the financing gap of the firm, which results from the balance constraint[9]. Therefore, assuming no quantity rationing, the credit market is in

---

8 Cf. D. Delli Gatti – M. Gallegati – L. Gardini (1993) for a similar analysis.

9 A diagrammatic representation of the demand and supply curves of finance would result as in the following note. In the $(F\text{-}\ i)$ space F^S is independent of the rate of interest, and shifts parametrically with changing levels of income and of the stock of debt. The curve F^D is downward sloping, because higher levels of the interest rate increase the opportunity cost of the alternative risk-free investment. The curve shifts upwards if, for given i, the current rate of profit increases, assuming that this determines an increase in the financial needs of the firm. For instance, if the increase in the rate of profit leads to an increase in the programmed investment expenditure which is higher than the firm's internal funds, this will determine an increase in the "financing gap" and in the demand for external funds, for a given rate of interest i.

equilibrium when the equilibrium condition for the other markets, that is, the goods and the money markets, is satisfied. This makes the credit market equilibrium condition redundant, and thus it is eliminated since it is not independent of the others[10].

Given equilibrium in the credit market, it is then possible to eliminate from condition [4.6^] the two components F^D and F^S on the right side and on the left side of the equation, respectively.

The following expression for the LM is thus obtained:

$$R + D = h(X, i). \qquad [4.6']$$

Hence, equation [4.6a] explains how the quantity of money existing in the economy is created, and the equilibrium condition between the demand and supply of money in equation [4.6'] explains the determination of the level of the rate of interest, given the state of liquidity preference.

The short-run equilibrium of the model is given, once again, by the IS-LM system. In comparison with the analysis of Chapter III, it has been broadened here to allow for the stock of money being an endogenous variable, through the analysis of the liquidity creation process via the channel of banking finance.

By taking into consideration the above points, the LM equation is finally modified in the following way:

---

10 The locus of points in the $(X - i)$ plane along which the credit market is in equilibrium is represented by a curve (PP) which is upward or downward sloping, depending on the effect (positive or negative, respectively) of income changes on the financing needs – and, correspondingly, on the demand for external funds (Cf. the previous note). In the diagram where the IS and LM curves are plotted, the PP curve may also be plotted for the credit market equilibrium. Yet, since the latter is not independent of the others, it will have to pass through the IS and LM curves' intersection point, because, for the Walras law, when the goods and the money markets are in equilibrium, the credit market will also be in equilibrium.

$$(R + D)pK = h(X/K, i),$$

or equivalently:

$$(R + D)K = [m\ (w/x)]\ h(X/K, i), \qquad [E2']$$

where D, the stock of accumulated debt, is the new variable which now figures in the broadened LM equation.

As to the equilibrium in the goods market, there are no relevant differences with the analysis made in Chapter III, apart from the consideration of the interest on debt (iD/p) which is charged to firms. This makes a difference between *gross* and *net* profits accruing to rentiers. The difference is exactly the amount of interest paid to banks. One may assume, to simplify the analysis, that the bankers' propensity to consume on the interest-income they receive is c_π, the same as the rentiers' propensity on their profit-income. Alternatively, one may assume that the interests received by banks are paid as dividends to workers, who have a propensity to consume on that income equal to c_π. This avoids adding complications as to the destination of income to consumption or investment. In fact, in this case the consumption function will be exactly the same one employed in equation [3.1], with the only difference that Π is now to be intended as the sum of net profit and interest on debt (iD), that is, gross (real) profits.

4.2 – Long-Run Equilibrium and Dynamics

The analysis is now extended to the consideration of the long-run equilibrium and dynamics of the model, in a similar way to the procedure developed for the basic model[11]. The equations which give the laws of motion for the exogenous variables are added to the short-run equilibrium relations, in order to "close" the system, thus leading to the complete dynamic model.

As will soon become evident, both *real* and *financial* determinants are at work in the enlarged model. In particular, as in model I the *real* determinant is represented by a "Classical" dynamic interaction mechanism between income distribution and the employment rate which, in a Keynesian perspective, feeds back to aggregate demand and the capacity utilisation rate. Moreover, the dynamics of debt is considered within this framework, thus allowing for *real* and *financial* determinants jointly in the analysis of macroeconomic behaviour[12].

In the previous Section a broader concept of the stock of money, which includes the liquidity created by the banking system, was introduced into the analysis. The consideration of finance brings about an important link between the *real* and *financial* sides of the economy, making money an endogenous variable. The cash flows of firms determine the conditions of access to credit, and since the behaviour of firms' cash flows is closely related to the aggregate economic performance in the cyclical process, it is possible to envisage a link between the liquidity creation process and the macroeconomic behaviour of the economy over time. It is important, therefore, to explain the working of these variables in the overall dynamics of the model.

When moving to a dynamic analysis, the evolution of the stock of debt D, which appears in equation [4.6'], has to be added to the system. In the short run

11 See Chapter III, Section 3.3.

12 In fact, in most contributions in the literature the *real* and the *financial* aspects of business cycles are treated separately. For instance, in M. Di Matteo (1984) and T. Asada (1989) the original Goodwin scheme (1967) is extended to consider money and prices, but there is no role for debt. In another class of models, which counts among others the important work by R. Franke - W. Semmler (1989), emphasis is placed instead on the financial determinants related to debt, drawing on Minsky's theoretical contribution. Yet, questions of distribution are not considered, here.

this is an exogenous variable, considered as given from the past. Its variation takes place gradually over time, through the flow of (new) finance. Hence, if equation [4.6a] is taken into account, given equilibrium in the credit market, the growth rate of nominal debt D may be expressed as:

$$\dot{D}/D \equiv F/D = \zeta\,[(X/K),\ (D/pK)]. \qquad \zeta_1 > 0,\ \zeta_2 < 0 \qquad [4.14']$$

At this point, equations [3.7] – [3.13], which have already been explained in Chapter III in the analysis of model I, may be employed here with minor changes, in order to complete the model. By setting $L \equiv (R+D)$, and $\Theta \equiv L/pK$, and by putting all equations together the following complete system is obtained:

$$C/K = (w/p)N/K + c_\pi\,[(X - (w/p)N]/K \qquad 0 < c_\pi < 1 \qquad [4.1]$$

$$I/K = \gamma[((X - (w/p)N)/K + \rho) - (i - \pi^e)] \qquad \gamma' > 0 \qquad [4.2]$$

$$N/K = (1/x)\,X/K, \qquad [4.3]$$

$$p = m\,(w/x), \qquad m > 1 \qquad [4.4]$$

$$X/K = C/K + I/K \qquad [4.5]$$

$$\Theta \equiv (L/pK) = h[(X/K),\ i] \qquad h_1 > 0;\ h_2 < 0 \qquad [4.6]$$

$$\dot{w}/w = f(N/N^S) + \dot{\pi}^e \qquad f' > 0 \qquad [4.7]$$

$$\frac{\dot{m}}{m} = -(\frac{1}{1+\xi})\left[\frac{\dot{w}}{w} - \frac{\dot{x}}{x}\right] + b(\Theta - \overline{\Theta}) \qquad \xi > 0,\ b > 0 \qquad [4.8]$$

$$x(t) = X(t)/N(t) = x(t_0)e^{\lambda(t-t_0)} \qquad [4.9]$$

$$\dot{\rho} = \alpha\,[\frac{X}{K}] \qquad \alpha' > 0 \qquad [4.10]$$

$$\dot{\pi}^e = \beta(\frac{\dot{p}}{p} - \pi^e) \qquad \beta > 0 \qquad [4.11]$$

$$\frac{\dot{\Theta}}{\Theta}=\frac{\dot{L}}{L}-\frac{\dot{p}}{p}-\frac{\dot{K}}{K} \qquad [4.12]$$

$$N^{S}(t)=N^{S}(t_0)e^{n(t-t_0)} \qquad [4.13]$$

$$\dot{L}/L=\phi\ [(X/K),\Theta]. \qquad \phi_1>0;\ \phi_2<0 \qquad [4.14]$$

The introduction of the (new) liquidity created through the banking financing process alters the characteristics of the stationary solution of the system and its behaviour over time.

In fact, now the following relation must hold in the long-run equilibrium:

$$\frac{\dot{\Theta}}{\Theta}=\frac{\dot{L}}{L}-\frac{\dot{p}}{p}-\frac{\dot{K}}{K}=0, \qquad [4.12\text{^}]$$

that is, with an accumulation proceeding at the natural or equilibrium rate:

$$\frac{\dot{\Theta}}{\Theta}=\frac{\dot{L}}{L}-\frac{\dot{p}}{p}-(n+\lambda)=0. \qquad [4.12\text{^^}]$$

This condition states that the (long-run) equilibrium growth rate of the "total" quantity of money L (in nominal terms), should equal the sum of the growth rates of prices and the stock of capital, the latter being the natural growth rate $(n + \lambda)$.

The analysis of the behaviour of the system off the steady state is now obviously influenced by the consideration of the motion of debt, in addition to the factors which have already been highlighted when referring to the dynamics of model I in Chapter III.

Equation [4.14] gives the behaviour of the overall liquidity L of the system in nominal terms, in relation to the level of output per unit of capital (*X/K*) and to the total stock of money in real terms Θ, which includes the stock of debt that is accumulated through the financing of firms. To the values of (*X/K*) and Θ at which condition [4.12^^] is satisfied, there corresponds the steady-state (equilibrium) growth rate of L.

It is possible to give a diagrammatic description of the behaviour of the system along the lines followed in Chapter III. Consider Figure (4.1).

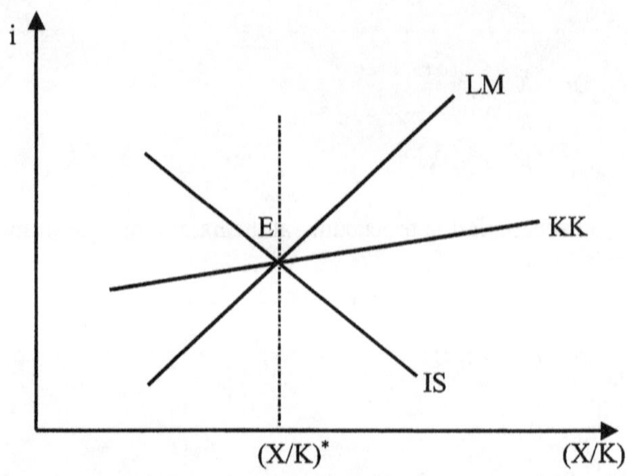

Figure 4.1. *The steady-state equilibrium in model II*

At point E in the graph the IS, LM and KK curves intersect and the system is at the steady-state "full" equilibrium position, with $X/K=(X/K)^*$, $\Theta=\Theta^*$, and with a flow of liquidity over time which satisfies equation [4.12^^].

For values of (*X/K*) above the equilibrium level, liquidity increases, and hence the growth rate of L exceeds the equilibrium rate, which is given in equation [4.12^^]; on the other hand, for above-equilibrium levels of the real stock of money Θ, which includes the stock of accumulated debt, the flow of liquidity decreases, and therefore L grows more slowly than the equilibrium rate.

Consider Figure (4.2), and suppose that the system is off the steady state, which is located at point E, and that the IS-LM equilibrium is at point A at the intersection of the IS_0 and LM_1 curves.

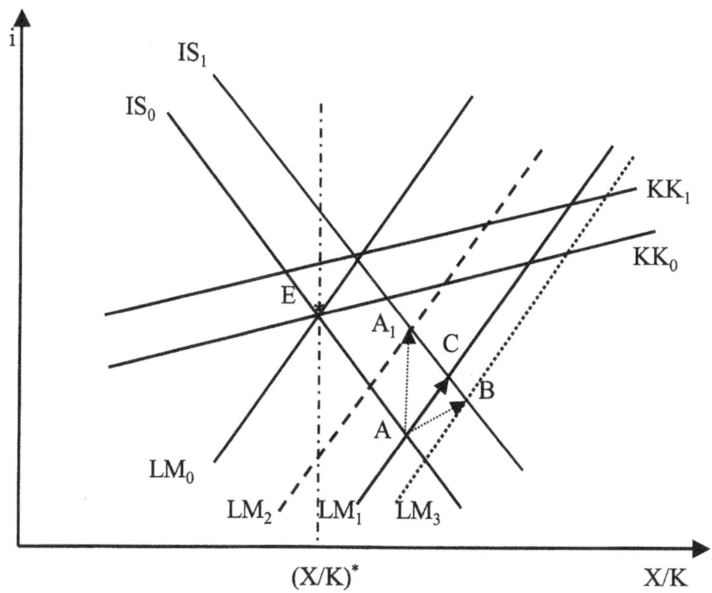

Figure 4.2. *The dynamics of model II*

Just as in the analysis developed in Chapter III, the system moves here according to the dynamic equations of the model, [4.1] – [4.14]. At point A the employment rate is above the equilibrium rate, with associated rising wages and prices, the wage-share is increasing and accumulation is proceeding faster than the natural rate. All this determines an euphoric "state of confidence", a general condition of "high spirits".

This performance of the "state of affairs" is reflected in an upwards shift of the IS and the KK curves[13] over time (towards the IS_1 and KK_1 curves, respectively), whereas the monetary equilibrium requires successive shifts to the left of the LM curve over time, towards intersections with the IS_1 at points like A_1 (as indicated by the dotted LM_2 curve).

The difference now is that the state of "vivacity" of the *real* side of the economy, that is, the positive performance of "fundamentals", is immediately transmitted to the *financial* side, in the form of an induced growth of the overall liquidity of the system through the flow of finance to firms, according to equation [4.14].

At point *A* the growth rate of debt, and thus, of overall liquidity, exceeds the equilibrium rate. In this case, the trajectory of the system might not lead to A_1, as it happened in the analysis of model I. In fact, if the growth rate of liquidity equals the sum of the rates at which prices and accumulation are growing, the LM curve need not shift over time, until the equilibrium condition of equation [4.12^^] is satisfied. Therefore, the upward shifts of the IS curve over time (IS_1) would take place along an LM curve which is not shifting (LM_1), so that the new intersections would be along a trajectory like the one leading to point *C*, as indicated by the arrow along the LM_1 curve.

In a state of financial "euphoria", the acceleration in the growth of liquidity may even be so pronounced that the LM curve is pushed further to the right over time (towards the dotted LM_3 curve), and so the trajectory of the system could lead to a point like point *B* (Figure (4.2)). In this case, the flow of liquidity created endogenously is capable of financing an accumulation process which

13 Cf. Chapter III.

proceeds at a higher rate than the natural rate, in the presence of a growth rate of prices which is also above the equilibrium rate.

Yet, as time goes by, the greater flow of finance, which has supported and enhanced the expansion of the economy, progressively leads to an increase in the firms' stock of debt too, and, consequently, to an expansion of the volume of total debt accumulating in the economy. Eventually, the worsening of the firms' financial cash flows increases their default-risk, thus affecting negatively the banks' attitude towards the supply of credit. The negative impact is soon reflected in a contraction of the growth rate of liquidity, as indicated by equation [4.14].

The monetary equilibrium required by condition [4.12^^] now implies rates of interest increasing over time, and an LM curve shifting towards the left over time.

When the IS, LM and KK curves intersect again, the adjustment process is not yet complete. As for model I, increasing growth rates of wages and therefore also of prices keep pushing the LM curve towards the left, and the wage-share increase keeps the IS curve moving upwards over time. Given stability, the shifts of the IS and LM curves would eventually bring the two curves to intersections above the KK curve. Now, the consideration of the endogeneity of liquidity adds some variations to the adjustment process. In fact, during the expansion process the overall liquidity of the system increases, since firms' cash flows are pro-cyclical. According to equation [4.14], the growth rate of liquidity increases for $X/K > (X/K)^*$. As explained above in relation to Figure (4.2), this could push the LM curve towards the right. As time elapses, and the expansion process proceeds, the overall amount of liquidity in the system Θ increases, since banks have satisfied the demand for finance from firms. In the late stage of the expansion, however, the supply of finance from the banking system starts shrinking and the slowdown in the growth rate of liquidity pushes the LM back towards the left over time.

The overall effect of the presence of endogenously created liquidity on the trajectory and thus on the stability of the system may vary. In fact, in some cases it may act as a stabilising mechanism keeping the economy away from a "burst". Consider, for instance, Figure (4.3).

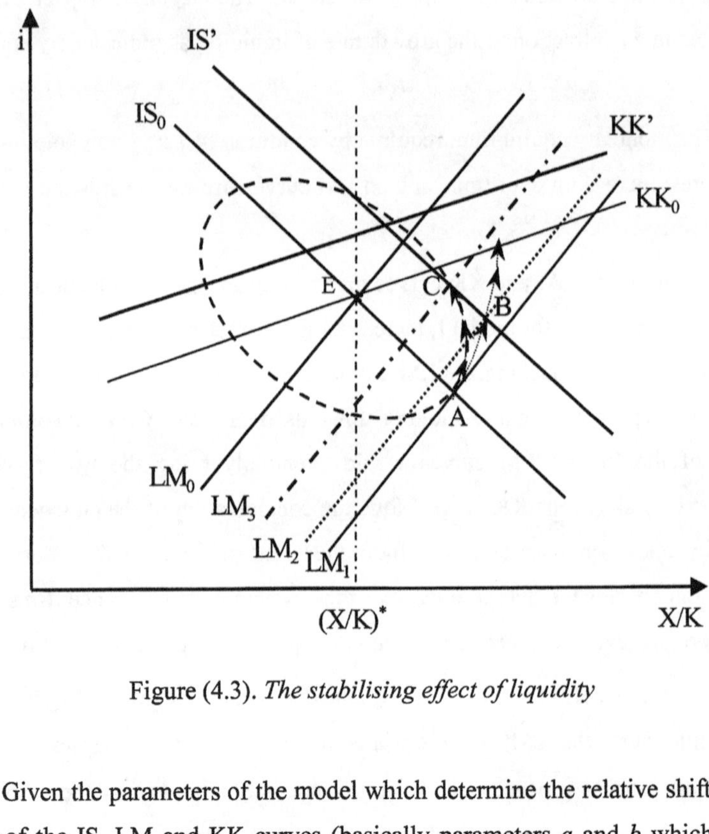

Figure (4.3). *The stabilising effect of liquidity*

Given the parameters of the model which determine the relative shifts over time of the IS, LM and KK curves (basically parameters *a* and *b* which were considered in Chapter III), liquidity might avoid instability by accelerating the shift to the left of the LM curve so that the trajectory of the system would be modified into the one going from point *A* to point *C*, that is to LM_3, instead of from point *A* to point *B*, that is to LM_2, thus curbing the expansion and avoiding the "burst".

Yet this is not the end of the story, since liquidity may turn out to be a destabilising factor as well. This can be understood by considering the diagram in Figure (4.4).

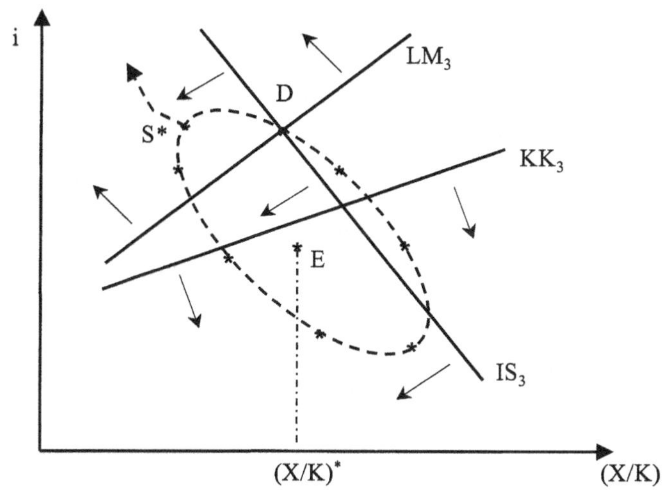

Figure 4.4. *The destabilising effect of liquidity*

Once the system has reached a point like the one in *D*, the trajectory might not reverse direction, because the LM curve keeps shifting leftwards. This could happen if at point *D* the volume of accumulated debt in the economy is so high (and the capacity utilisation rate so low) that a strong contraction in the creation of liquidity occurs. This would mean that, in this case, the growth rate of liquidity is falling, and moreover it is smaller than the growth rates of prices and accumulation, although these have returned to their equilibrium values. Therefore, according to equation [4.14] the LM keeps shifting to the left over time (for instance, towards point *S*), with very high interest rates and low levels of the output-capital ratio.

Moreover, if the system is at point *D* the negative effect on the "state of confidence" and expectations could actually depress the accumulation process and thus delay, or even compromise the recovery, with the IS_3 and the KK_3 curve shifting downwards over time.

Hence, at a point like point *S*, in which the system is far from the steady-state equilibrium, liquidity could have a destabilising effect and the trajectory of the system could be divergent[14]. In contrast, given stability, when enough time has passed, the system recovers from the depression; this, however, might happen after the system has experimented a strong deflation and a long stagnation, in the absence of any "control".

It is possible to examine some aspects of the stability of the model in more detail, proceeding along the lines of the analysis of model I in Chapter III. Leaving aside ρ and π^e, a system of three differential equations is obtained, and the fundamental system is given in the following:

$$\dot{m}/m = -a[f(E) - \lambda] + b(\Theta - \overline{\Theta})$$
$$\dot{E}/E = \dot{y}/y + g(m, \Theta) - (n + \lambda) \qquad [S2]$$
$$\dot{\Theta}/\Theta = [\phi_0 + \phi_1[(1 - 1/m)y - (1 - 1/\overline{m})\overline{y}] - \phi_2(\Theta - \overline{\Theta})] - \dot{p}/p - g(m, \overline{\Theta})$$

where, in the third equation, the evolution of the money stock *L* in nominal terms is expressed as the sum of a constant quantity ϕ_0, and of a variable

14 The overall behaviour depends, of course, on the attitude of the banking system towards the supply of credit, and hence, on the values of $\varphi_1 > 0$; $\varphi_2 < 0$ in equation [4.14].

quantity. The latter is linked positively to the difference between the firms' rate of current profit $[(1-1/m)y]$ and its normal (or average) value, and negatively to the difference between the current level of Θ and its normal (or average) level.

The local behaviour of the system is examined through a linearisation around the steady-state equilibrium of system [S2]. In addition to the factors which have already emerged in the analysis of model I, the dynamic behaviour of the model is now influenced by *financial* determinants. In particular, a strong sensitivity of the growth rate of the "total" money stock L to the behaviour of the firms' profit rate may act as a stabilising factor in the model. This case occurs if ϕ_1 is relatively large. On the other hand, a relatively strong sensitivity of the growth rate of L to the total stock of real debt may increase the degree of instability, and this happens if ϕ_2 is relatively large.

The interpretation of this point is that employing a broader concept of money, which includes banking finance, introduces an endogenous component in the growth rate of money. Its peculiarity appears precisely in its two-fold nature during the cyclical process. It is "credit", and hence a "leverage" factor supporting the accumulation process and enhancing growth but, at the same time, it is also "debt" and hence the factor determining the financial structure of the firm (the leverage ratio), thus acting as a possible source of instability.

CONCLUSIONS

The overview of the literature on endogenous business cycles presented in the first part of the work highlighted some of the basic mechanisms that govern the dynamic processes of modern capitalist economies, leading to fluctuations in economic activity and to a series of regularities known as "stylised facts". In particular, one class of models emphasizes the *real* determinants of cycles, due to either the dynamic interaction between the employment rate and income distribution, starting from the Goodwin model (1967) up to more recent contributions (Di Matteo (1984) and Asada (1989)), or to the *multiplier-accelerator*–type mechanisms, drawing on Hicks's contribution (1950). Another class of models stresses the role of *financial* dynamics in business cycles, in particular the role of the endogenous liquidity creation process and the motion of debt, along the Keynesian tradition which goes back to Minsky and develops further in light of the theoretical insights coming from the New Keynesian research.

The central part of the present work deals, first, with the development of a basic set up for a macrodynamic growth model (model I), in which the "Classical" mechanism based on the feed back between changes in income distribution and the employment rate is extended to the performance of aggregate demand and the capacity utilisation rate over the cycle.

The model is then broadened in order to take into consideration the liquidity creation process through the banking system and the analysis of debt, financial fragility and systemic risk over the cycle. This extension (model II) aims to add the *financial* dynamics to the *real* factors governing the cycle, which are the only factors at work in model I.

The explanation of the *real* dynamics of the model is based fundamentally on the existence of a two-fold mechanism linking the rate of profit of firms to the accumulation process. On the one side there is the "Classical" interdependence between variations in income distribution and the accumulation process, which is present in the Goodwin model (1967), according to which a decrease in the profit-share and correspondingly an increase in the wage-share reduces investment and, hence, the employment rate, thus inducing eventually a fall in the wage-share and a recovery of investment. This dynamic interaction is the well known predator-prey relationship. The second component of the mechanism which is considered here, and is not present in that kind of model, is the interaction between the dynamics of income distribution and the performance of aggregate demand and the capacity utilisation rate over time.

The existence of this two-fold mechanism stems from the peculiar nature of wages, which are the price of a production factor, and thus a cost for the firm, but at the same time they are also the income accruing to workers, and thus a source of the demand for firms' output. This is, indeed, one fundamental intuition of Keynes, and a rather revolutionary concept in economic theory – in comparison with the mainstream economic theory up to that time.

As to the role of effective demand in the cyclical process, in the model the full utilisation of the capital stock is not always attained and this influences firms' pricing strategies and the dynamics of income distribution over the cycle. In short, given the (pro-cyclical) variations in costs, the behaviour of firms as to the mark-up over costs is, fundamentally, aimed to keep the market-share of their own product constant, within the context of imperfectly competitive markets. In fact, it is well known that, whereas in perfectly competitive markets firms face an infinitely elastic demand curve, on the contrary, in oligopolistic markets, as Kalecki himself had earlier emphasized (1954), firms are primarily concerned with the rate of capacity utilisation and the market-share, under conditions of uncertainty about demand and competitors' behaviour. These factors have a relevant role in firms' pricing strategies and in the dynamics of income distribution.

The specification of the equation for price variations over time is made taking into account two factors. First of all, in light of the argument above, it is assumed that firms do not transfer completely onto prices the changes occurring in costs over time, within the context of imperfectly competitive markets. Since firms' "direct costs" move pro-cyclically, this factor works in the sense of making the firms' mark-up counter-cyclical, and hence income distribution counter-cyclical.

However, this is not the only factor at work in the behaviour of prices and in the dynamics of income distribution. It is assumed that variations in prices are also influenced "directly" by the demand pressure. This is signalled by the behaviour of real liquidity, which is thus supposed to indicate the demand equipped with purchasing power, and hence to capture the "state of demand". The idea is that the availability of liquidity encourages expenditure, whereas the shortage of purchasing power discourages it. So firms tend to restore their profit margins in periods of abundant money and high spending, whereas they let them fall in periods of scarce liquidity and low spending.

Altogether, the behaviour of prices and distribution over time is the resultant of the two components mentioned above: on the one side, the *cost-pressure*, which is influenced by demand uncertainty and market structure constraints that lead to the choice of "trading-off" a constant market-share with the variability in margins; on the other side, the "direct" effect of the *demand-pressure*.

Since changes in distribution affect the level of aggregate demand and the associated rate of capacity utilisation in the model, when income distribution and employment fluctuate aggregate demand and capacity utilisation also fluctuate, thus influencing the behaviour of "direct costs" which then feeds back to the dynamics of income distribution.

It is quite evident that the higher the state of uncertainty of firms about the demand for their output and their competitors' strategies, which is more typical in concentrated markets, the higher the need for firms to "trade-off" profit margins with the capacity utilisation rate. And consequently, the larger the variations in income-shares and the associated effects on the level of aggregate demand and on the capacity utilisation rate.

In the analysis of the dynamic behaviour of the model it emerges that the stability properties of the system depend on the value of the parameters which are present in the equations that give the law of motion of prices and accordingly the law of motion of margins over time. These parameters reflect the constraint of the market structure and the role of the demand pressure on firms' pricing strategies. The higher the state of uncertainty under which firms operate, the higher the degree of *inertia* in the adjustment of prices to variations occurring in costs over time, and consequently, the larger the variations in income distribution over the cycle. And the higher the possibility of the system losing stability.

In the final part of the work the model is broadened to include an endogenous concept of liquidity. This aims to take into consideration *real* and *financial* mechanisms jointly into the analysis of the economic process. Following the literature on financial dynamics in business cycles, it is assumed that the liquidity creation process is pro-cyclical and is closely related to the macroeconomic performance. In particular, the supply of finance by banks depends on the evolution of the firms' cash flows over time, so that the growth rate of liquidity is positively related to the profit rate and negatively related to the stock of accumulated debt. The latter stems from the Kaleckian assumption of "increasing risk" associated with the rising leverage of firms. Consequently, expansionary phases are characterised by increasing flow of (new) liquidity, due to "well-behaving" cash flows, and unutilised margins of "borrowing capacity". As time passes, the incentive to a debt-supported accumulation process determines an increase in the stock of total debt in the system. In the later stages of an expansion, then, the level of debt acts negatively on the attitude of banks towards the financing of the economy. Therefore, a sharp fall in the overall liquidity might occur. Altogether, the behaviour of the model will depend on the reaction of the banking system towards the deterioration of cash flows and the increasing leverage of the system, which determine the terms at which the demand for finance is satisfied.

The consideration of a broader concept of money by including the endogenous liquidity creation process proves to be a factor that supports and enhances the accumulation process, thus stimulating growth. At the same time, because of the two-fold nature of finance, that is, it being "debt" as well as "credit", the liquidity creation process itself might act negatively on the accumulation process, leading to financial instability which may be easily transmitted to the *real* side of the economy. If the level of debt is considered excessively high with respect to the physiological level (according to the evaluation made by banks), a sharp fall in liquidity and a collapse in the accumulation process might occur.

In conclusion, the work aims to single out in the behaviour of firms an essential link in the cyclical process, given the assumption of imperfectly competitive markets. In the model firms define their pricing strategies taking into account the effects on the level of aggregate demand and the rate of capacity utilisation. The behaviour of firms ultimately determines the dynamics of income distribution, given the changes in costs over time, and this feeds back to the performance of aggregate demand and to the capacity utilisation rate in the cyclical process.

Emphasis is also placed on the role of *financial* factors, in particular on the endogenous liquidity creation process through the bank financing of firms and the related motion of debt. The stress is on the two-fold nature of "finance": it supports the accumulation process and enhances growth, and yet, it can lead to financial fragility and act as a possible source of systemic instability. In this way, the *financial* factors interact with the above *real* mechanisms and deeply affect the overall macrodynamics of the model.

APPENDIX A

A.1 – Some Notes on the Nature of Non-Linear Systems of Differential Equations and their Applications to the Study of Economic Fluctuations

(Cf. Chapter II, note 13).

Consider a simple second-order differential equation:

$$\ddot{y} + \alpha\dot{y} + y = 0,$$

where y is the deviation of a variable from the equilibrium position. It is well known that the solution to the equation is a curve that describes harmonic oscillations, and that its amplitude depends on the sign of parameter α: if $\alpha > 0$ the amplitude of the oscillations is decreasing over time, and eventually the cycle dampens, if $\alpha < 0$ the amplitude increases and the oscillations tend to explode and if $\alpha = 0$ the oscillations are of constant amplitude.

It is possible to modify the differential equation in order to "control" the dynamics of the cycle, so that dampening or exploding oscillations are avoided, and hence the system exhibits persistent oscillations. This effect was obtained by B. van der Pol[1], by introducing a positive "resistance" which increases with the amplitude of the oscillations.

1 The study was presented in 1928 at the meeting of the "Batavian Society of Logical Empirical Philosophy" and the utility of its application to the analysis of business cycles was soon recognised by the Dutch economist L. Hamburger ["Note on economic cycles and relaxation-oscillations"]. The theory of oscillations was studied almost contemporaneously by A. Liénard and by Ph. Le Corbeiller. On the applications of the theory of nonlinear oscillations to dynamic systems in economics cf. G. Gandolfo (1996).

The van der Pol equation is the following:

$$\ddot{y} + \alpha(y^2 - 1)\dot{y} + y = 0$$

where the "resistance" is represented by the coefficient of $\dot{y}$ and is a non-linear function of y. For $\alpha > 0$ the cycle no longer disappears; as α increases, then, the amplitude of the oscillations increases suddenly, and they tend immediately to a non-exploding cycle. For large values of the parameter, the "shape" describing the solution to the equation repeats itself over time, i.e. a limit cycle exists. A necessary condition in order to have a stable limit cycle is that $\alpha > 0$. For $\alpha < 0$ the limit cycle is unstable, if it exists, and it disappears as times increases.

Moreover, the effect of this "resistance" is to produce asymmetrical, non-sinusoidal cycles. These kind of oscillations are also known as "relaxation oscillations". In the van der Pol equation one endogenous nonlinearity is both a necessary and sufficient condition for the existence of turning points.

A generalisation of the van der Pol equation is represented by the Liénard equation, in which the "resistance" is introduced in the form of a function, $f(x)$, so that the differential equation above becomes:

$$\ddot{x} + f(x)\dot{x} + g(x) = 0.$$

If functions $f(x)$ and $g(x)$ satisfy specific conditions, the Liénard equation has one closed orbit, which is a limit cycle Γ that in the phase plane surrounds the origin. Moreover, as $t \to \infty$ all the other orbits in the neighbourhood approach this limit cycle Γ. The following conditions have to be satisfied[2]:

2 For a proof, see G. F. Simmons (1972).

- both functions $f(x)$ and $g(x)$ are continuous and have continuous derivatives for all x ;
- $g(x)$ is an odd function such that $g(x) > 0$, for $x > 0$, and $f(x)$ is an even function;
- the function $F(x) = \int_0^x f(x)dx$ has to satisfy the following conditions: it must have one positive root at $x = a$, be negative for $0 < x < a$ and positive and nondecreasing for $x > a$, and tend to infinity as $x \to \infty$.

In some cases it is possible to model business cycles in the form of a Liénard-van der Pol equation, and this allows to verify easily if the conditions for the existence of a limit cycle are satisfied. This is the case of the Kaldor model (1940) in the Chang-Smith (1971) reformulation, illustrated in Section A.4.

A.2 – On the Notion of Limit Cycles. The Poincarè-Benedixson Theorem

(Cf. Chapter II, note 13)

The notion of limit-cycle can be formalised in the following terms (cf. Beltrami, 1987). Given the system:

$$\dot{\mathbf{x}} = f(\mathbf{x}), \quad \mathbf{x} \text{ in } \Re^2, \qquad \text{[A.1]}$$

the set of all curves starting from different points which are solution to system [A.1] is called a "flow" of the system. The path of system [A.1] is also called an *orbit.* Define the *positive limiting set* γ^+ the set of points $\boldsymbol{\rho}$ in $\Re^2$, which satisfy the following:

$$\left\|\mathbf{x}(t_n) - \boldsymbol{\rho}\right\| \rightarrow \mathbf{0}, \quad \text{as } n \rightarrow \infty,$$

where $\{t_n\}$is an increasing sequence of time. A *cycle* or a *closed orbit* γ is a trajectory that returns periodically to a point $\boldsymbol{\rho}$ (that is, there are periodic solutions to system [A.1]). An orbit γ is said to tend to a *limit cycle* Γ if $\gamma^+ = \Gamma$ and if Γ is a non-constant closed orbit. The Poincarè-Benedixson theorem in weak form may be stated as follows [cf. Hirsch-Smale (1974), p.248; Dore (1993), p.150]:

- Let γ be an orbit starting in **Ω,** which is the set of all orbits of system [A.1]. Then, its positive limiting set γ^+ is nonempty, and if it contains no equilibria of the system, either γ is a cycle or γ^+ is a limit cycle.
- If Ω contains no cycles but does contain one single attracting point $\boldsymbol{\rho}$, then $\gamma^+ = \boldsymbol{\rho}$.

The theorem may be illustrated graphically by considering the two figures below A.1(1) and A.1(2) [Cf. Dore (1993), p. 151]. The first figure represents the case in which Ω contains one unstable equilibrium $\bar{\mathbf{x}}$ and all orbits in its neighbourhood diverge from it: in this case $\bar{\mathbf{x}}$ is a repelling point. The set which is obtained by removing point $\bar{\mathbf{x}}$ from Ω contains a limit cycle Γ, and as time goes to infinity all orbits "inside" and "outside" it converge to Γ. In figure A.1(2) $\bar{\mathbf{x}}$ is a single stable equilibrium point, that is, an "attractor", and all orbits in the neighbourhood approach it.

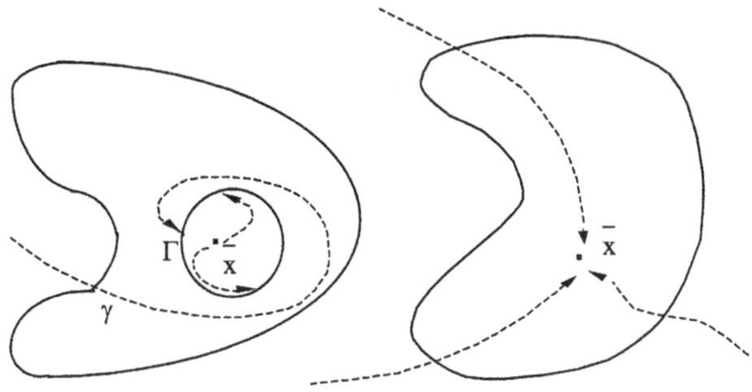

Figure A.1(1) Figure A.1(2)

A.3 – A Proof of the Existence of a Limit Cycle in Goodwin (1951)

(Cf. Chapter II, note 15)

The existence of a limit cycle may be proved by considering the *Jacobian* of the reduced form of system [2.6], evaluated at the equilibrium point:

$$J = \begin{bmatrix} \frac{\eta\gamma}{1-\beta} & \frac{-\eta}{1-\beta} \\ \eta\gamma & 1-\eta \end{bmatrix} .$$

In order to get an unstable vortex the discriminant of the characteristic equation $P(x) = x^2 - (tr\ J)\ x + det\ J = 0$ must be negative, which implies that condition $4\ det\ J > (tr\ J)^2$ is satisfied.

Moreover, it is necessary that the *Jacobian* is greater than unity. This is equivalent to setting $\eta > \eta * = (1 - \beta) / \gamma$, where $\eta *$ is the critical value of the control parameter η, which is given for *det* $J(\eta^*) = 1$. This condition is generally satisfied, given the economic meaning of the parameters, whereas for the first condition to be satisfied it is necessary to find a range of values for η which includes η^*, within which the discriminant is negative.

A.4 – On the Existence of a Limit Cycle in the Kaldor Model

(Cf. Chapter II, note 17).

Recall the Chang-Smith reformulation of the Kaldor model:

$$I = I(y, k);\; S = S(y, k), \quad I_y > 0,\; S_y > 0,\; S_k > 0\;;\; I_k < 0\;;\; I_y > S_y;\; I_k > S_k \quad [2.7]$$

$$\mu \dot{y} = I(y,k) - S(y,k) \quad [2.8]$$

$$\dot{k} = \bar{I}(y,k). \quad [2.9]$$

From equation [2.8] it results:

$$k = \psi(y, \dot{y}) \quad [2.10]$$

and correspondingly the implicit function $F(k, y, \dot{y}) = 0$. By resorting to the implicit function theorem it then follows:

$$\frac{\partial k}{\partial y} = -\frac{F_y}{F_k} = \psi_y = \frac{S_y - I_y}{I_k - S_k} \quad [2.11]$$

$$\frac{\partial k}{\partial \dot{y}} = -\frac{F_{\dot{y}}}{F_k} = \psi_{\dot{y}} = \frac{-\mu}{I_k - S_k}. \quad [2.12]$$

By differentiating equation [2.10]:

$$\dot{k} = \psi_y \dot{y} + \psi_{\dot{y}} \ddot{y} = \bar{I}(y,k)$$

and by taking into account equations [2.11] and [2.12], after simplifications the following form is obtained:

$$\ddot{y} + \frac{1}{\mu}\left[I_y - S_y\right]\dot{y} + \frac{1}{\mu}\left[I_k - S_k\right]\bar{I}(y,k) = 0.$$

If equation [2.9] is substituted into the expression above, variable k is dropped, thus yielding:

$$\ddot{y} + \frac{1}{\mu}\left[I_y - S_y\right]\dot{y} + \frac{1}{\mu}\left[I_k - S_k\right] h(y,\dot{y}) = 0 \qquad [2.13]$$

where $\bar{I}\left[y,\psi(y,\dot{y})\right] \equiv h(y,\dot{y})$. Equation [2.13] is a Liénard-van der Pol equation of the type:

$$\ddot{y} + f(y)\dot{y} + g(y) = 0,$$

where $f(y) = \frac{1}{\mu}\left[I_y - S_y\right]$ and $g(y) = \frac{1}{\mu}\left[I_k - S_k\right] h(y,\dot{y})$.

Given the assumptions on the functions which have been made above, equation [2.13] has at least one limit cycle[3].

---

3 Cf. M. Dore (1993); G. Gandolfo (1996).

A.5 –Analytical Details on the Asada Model

(Cf. Chapter II, note 24).

The stationary solution of the system is given by:[4]

$$Z_n^* = H^{-1}(h + n_1 + n_2),$$
$$E^* = f^{-1}(n_2),$$
$$m^* = \pi^{-1}\left|\left(\frac{\mu + \alpha(\Phi^* - \bar{i}) - (n_1 + n_2)}{1-\alpha}\right)\right|_{Z_n = Z_n^*}, \quad \Phi^* \equiv \Phi(Z_n^*)$$

and by linearising system [2.22] around the equilibrium point yields:

$$\begin{vmatrix} \dot{Z}_n \\ \dot{E} \\ \dot{m} \end{vmatrix} = \begin{vmatrix} 0 & F_{12}^* & 0 \\ F_{21}^* & 0 & 0 \\ F_{31}^* & 0 & F_{33}^* \end{vmatrix} \begin{vmatrix} Z_n - Z_n^* \\ E - E^* \\ m - m^* \end{vmatrix} \quad \text{where:} \quad \begin{aligned} &F_{12}^* \equiv f'(E^*)Z_n^* > 0; \\ &F_{21}^* \equiv H'(z_n^*)E^* < 0; \\ &F_{31}^* \equiv [\alpha \underset{(+/0)}{i_1^*} - \underset{(-)}{\pi_1^*} - \underset{(-)}{H'(Z_n^*)}]; \\ &F_{33}^* \equiv (\alpha - \underset{(-)}{1})\pi_2^* m^*. \end{aligned}$$

The roots of the characteristic equations are, then:

$$\lambda = F_{33}^*; \quad \pm\sqrt{F_{12}^* F_{21}^*};$$

$$= (\alpha - 1)\pi_2{}^* m^*; \quad \pm i\sqrt{-\underset{(-)}{H'(Z_n^*)}\underset{(+)}{f'(E^*)}Z_n{}^* E^*}, \text{ where } i \equiv \sqrt{-1}.$$

---

4 Cf. T. Asada (1989).

APPENDIX B

B.1 – A Simplified Presentation of the Basic Model. IS-LM Equilibrium and Comparative-Statics

Consider, to simplify as far as possible the analysis, the following explicit form for function I/K:

$$I / K = g_0 + g(r - i)$$

where g is now a coefficient. If the rate of profit r is made explicit by expressing it as the product of the profit-share and the output-capital ratio, that is as $r \equiv (\Pi / X) \cdot (X / K) = (1\text{-}1/m)\, y$, then I/K can be turned into:

$$I / K = g_0 + g\big((1 - 1/m)y - i\big). \qquad [B.1]$$

Consider, then, a linear form for the demand for money function (in real terms):

$$M^D / pK = h_0 y - h_1 i .$$

The IS-LM system is, thus, constituted by the following two equations:

$$\begin{aligned} s(1 - 1/m)y &= g\big((1 - 1/m)y - i\big) + A \\ H &= h_0 y - h_1 i \end{aligned} \qquad [B.2]$$

where A stands for the autonomous component of expenditure. The solution to system [B.2] yields the expressions for y^* and i^* which represent the short-run equilibrium of the model:

$$y^* = \frac{gH + h_1 A}{(s-g)(1-1/m)h_1 + (gh_0)};$$

$$i^* = \frac{h_0 A - ((s-g)(1-1/m)H)}{(s-g)(1-1/m)h_1 + (gh_0)}.$$

Thus the solution of y is of the form $y^* = Y(m, H, A)$ and the solution of i is of the form $i^* = i(m, H, A)$.

To answer the typical question addressed in statics, that is, which is the response of each endogenous variable (y and i, respectively) to a "jump" in the exogenous variables (m and H, leaving aside A for the moment), that occurs at a given time, it is convenient to consider a linear approximation of system [B.2] by totally differentiating around the equilibrium point (y^*, i^*):

$$\begin{aligned} &[(s-g)(1-1/m)]dy + gdi + [(s-g)y(1/m^2)]dm - dA = 0 \\ &dH = h_0 dy - h_1 di \end{aligned} \qquad \text{[B.2a]}$$

which lead to the two partial derivatives of y with respect to the exogenous variables m and H:

$$Y_m \equiv \partial y / \partial m = -\frac{(s-g)(1/m^2)h_1 y}{Z}$$

$$Y_H \equiv \partial y / \partial H = \frac{g}{Z},$$

where $Z \equiv (s-g)(1-1/m)h_1 + gh_0$. The sign of the two expressions depend on the denominator Z, which is positive if the IS curve is downward sloping or if it is upward sloping but flatter than the LM curve[1]. If $Z > 0$ is assumed, then the signs of the two expressions above are:

$$Y_m < 0; \; Y_H > 0.$$

The partial derivatives of i may also be determined from system [B.2a]:

$$i_m \equiv \partial i / \partial m = -\frac{h_0 (s-g)(1/y)(1/m^2)}{Z},$$

$$i_H \equiv \partial i / \partial H = -\frac{(s-g)(1-1/m)}{Z};$$

which are both negative if $Z > 0$. If equation [B.1] is considered once again, the partial derivatives for function $I/K = g(m, H)$ may then be calculated easily as follows:

$$g_m \equiv \partial g / \partial m = g[(1-1/m)\partial y / \partial m + (1/m^2)y - \partial i / \partial m],$$

$$g_H \equiv \partial g / \partial H = g[(1-1/m)\partial y / \partial H - \partial i / \partial H]$$

which are both positive, if the signs of the partial derivatives of y and of i are as above. Therefore, it follows that:

---

1 This point can be explained easily by considering that $Z \equiv (s-g)(1-1/m)h_1 + gh_0 > 0$ implies $-[(s-g)(1-1/m)/g] < h_0 / h_1$. It is easy to proof that the expression to the left side of the inequality symbol corresponds to the slope of the IS curve, whereas the expression to the right corresponds to the slope of the LM curve.

$g_m > 0; \quad g_H > 0.$

Consider, now, the (short-run) equilibrium solution for y given by the IS-LM system, in terms of the exogenous variables of the model:

$y = Y(m, H).$

If the logarithmic differentiation is carried out:

$$\frac{dy}{y} = Y_m \frac{dm}{m} + Y_H \frac{dH}{H}$$

and if both sides of the expression above are divided by dt, then by setting $dy/dt \equiv \dot{y}$; $dm/dt \equiv \dot{m}$ and $dH/t \equiv \dot{H}$, the following expression is obtained:

$$\frac{\dot{y}}{y} = Y_m \frac{\dot{m}}{m} + Y_H \frac{\dot{H}}{H}$$

where remember $Y_m \equiv \partial Y(m,H)/\partial m$ and $Y_H \equiv \partial Y(m,H)/\partial H$.

B.2 – Steady-State Equilibrium and Dynamics

In order to reduce the "size" of the system, the model has been simplified as far as possible, by dropping the variables ρ, the "state of confidence", and π^e, the expected rate of price inflation. The following system is, thus, obtained:

$$\dot{m}/m = -a[f(E)-\lambda] + b(H-\overline{H})$$
$$\dot{E}/E = \dot{y}/y + g(m,H) - (n+\lambda) \qquad [S1]$$
$$\dot{H}/H = \mu - \dot{p}/p - g(m,H)$$

where $y \equiv X/K$, $a \equiv \xi/(1+\xi)$ and $g(m,H) \equiv \dot{K}/K$.

Remember the expression for the growth rate of prices $\dot{p}/p$ which was given in equation [3.8'] in Chapter III:

$$\frac{\dot{p}}{p} = (1-a)\left[\frac{\dot{w}}{w} - \frac{\dot{x}}{x}\right] + b(H-\overline{H}) =$$
$$= (1-a)[f(E)-\lambda] + b(H-\overline{H})$$

and recall the expression for $\dot{y}/y$ which was obtained in Section B.1 of the present Appendix. Then system [S1] may be reformulated in terms of the three variables *m, E, H*, thus yielding the following fundamental system:

[S1a]:

$$\dot{m} = \{-a[f(E)-\lambda] + b(H-\overline{H}\}m \equiv F_1(m,E,H);$$
$$\dot{E} = \{Y_m[-a[f(E)-\lambda]+b(H-\overline{H})] + Y_H[\mu-(1-a)[f(E)-\lambda]-b(H-\overline{H})-g(m,H)] +$$
$$+g(m,H)-(n+\lambda)\}E \equiv F_2(m,E,H);$$
$$\dot{H} = \{\mu-(1-a)[f(E)-\lambda]-b(H-\overline{H})-g(m,H)\}H \equiv F_3(m,E,H).$$

It is possible to have information about the "local" behaviour of the system by carrying out a linearisation of system [S1a] around the equilibrium point. It is assumed that an economically meaningful stationary solution, that is a long-run equilibrium, exists. Hence, first the stationary solution is determined by calculating the values m^*, E^* and H^* which are the solution to the following system:

$$\begin{aligned} \dot{m} &\equiv F_1(m,E,H)=0 \\ \dot{E} &\equiv F_2(m,E,H)=0 \\ \dot{H} &\equiv F_3(m,E,H)=0. \end{aligned} \qquad \text{[S1*]}$$

Then, the *Jacobian* is calculated, that is, the matrix of the partial derivatives of the above functions F_i (i = 1, 2, 3), evaluated at the equilibrium point.

After the linearisation, system [S1] may also be written in the following compact form:

$$\begin{bmatrix} \dot{m} \\ \dot{E} \\ \dot{H} \end{bmatrix} = \begin{bmatrix} F_{11}^* & F_{12}^* & F_{13}^* \\ F_{21}^* & F_{22}^* & F_{23}^* \\ F_{31}^* & F_{32}^* & F_{33}^* \end{bmatrix} \cdot \begin{bmatrix} m-m^* \\ E-E^* \\ H-H^* \end{bmatrix} \qquad \text{[S1']}$$

where F_{ij}^* denotes the partial derivative of F_i. The expressions corresponding to the elements F_{ij}^* in matrix J are:

$F_{11}^* = 0$;

$F_{12}^* = -\, a f'(E^*)\, m^*$;

$F_{13}^* = b\, m^*$;

$F_{21}^* = \{Y_H^*(-g_m^*) + g_m^*\} E* = \{-g_m^*(Y_H^* - 1)\} E^*$;

$F_{22}^* = \{Y_m^*(-a) f'(E^*) - Y_H^*(1-a) f'(E^*)\}\, E^*$;

$$F_{23}^{*} = \{Y_{m}^{*} b - Y_{H}^{*}(b + g_{H}^{*}) + g_{H}^{*}\}E^{*} = \{b(Y_{m}^{*} - Y_{H}^{*}) - g_{H}^{*}(Y_{H}^{*} - 1)\}E^{*};$$

$$F_{31}^{*} = -g_{m}^{*} H^{*};$$

$$F_{32}^{*} = \{-(1-a)f'(E^{*})\}H^{*};$$

$$F_{33}^{*} = \{-(b + g_{H}^{*})\}H^{*}.$$

The Routh-Hurwicz conditions for stability are:

(i) $a_2 = (-\text{tr}\, J) > 0;$
(ii) $a_1 = (\Sigma\, \text{principal minors of}\, J) > 0;$
(iii) $a_0 = (-\det J) > 0;$
(iv) $a_1 a_2 - a_0 > 0.$

These provide that the roots of the third-order characteristic equation $\lambda^3 + a_2\lambda^2 + a_1\lambda + a_0 = 0$ have all negative real part.

If the conditions (*i*)-(*iii*) are all three satisfied, whereas (*iv*) is not, the system admits a pair of imaginary roots, and thus there are periodic solutions, if $a_1 a_2 - a_0 = 0$. The system has, instead, one root with negative real part and two roots with positive real part if $a_1 a_2 - a_0 < 0$, and in this case the system is unstable.

To verify the stability conditions of the system the signs of the F_{ij}^{*} in the *Jacobian* matrix have to be determined. It is easy to prove that[2] :

$F_{11}^{*} = 0$; $F_{12}^{*} < 0$; $F_{13}^{*} > 0$;

2 The conditions obtained are valid under the assumption of a downward sloping IS curve, or an upward sloping IS curve but flatter than the LM curve. In these cases, the following signs were obtained (cf. Appendix B.1): $Y_H > 0$, $Y_m < 0$, $g_H > 0$, $g_m > 0$.

$$F_{21}^{*} < 0, \text{ if } Y_{H}^{*} > 1; \; F_{22}^{*} < 0, \text{ if } a < \frac{Y_{H}^{*}}{Y_{H}^{*} - Y_{m}^{*}}; \; F_{23}^{*} < 0, \text{ if } Y_{H}^{*} > 1; \qquad [B.3]$$

$$F_{31}^{*} < 0; \quad F_{32}^{*} < 0; \quad F_{33}^{*} < 0.$$

At this point, the Routh-Hurwicz criterion given with conditions (*i*)-(*iv*) can be examined in detail.

Coefficient a_2 corresponds to the negative value of the trace of matrix *J*. Therefore, in model I the following result is obtained:

$$a_2 = -[\underset{(-)}{F_{22}^{*}} + \underset{(-)}{F_{33}^{*}}] =$$
$$= -\left\{[Y_{m}^{*}(-a)f'(E^{*}) - Y_{H}^{*}(1-a)f'(E^{*})]E^{*} - (b + g_{H}^{*})H^{*}\right\}$$

which is positive, if $a < \frac{Y_{H}^{*}}{Y_{H}^{*} - Y_{m}^{*}}$.

Coefficient a_2 is identical with the sum of the principal minors of matrix *J*. Its value is then given by:

$$a_2 = -[\underset{(-)}{F_{22}^{*}} + \underset{(-)}{F_{33}^{*}}] =$$
$$= -\left\{[Y_{m}^{*}(-a)f'(E^{*}) - Y_{H}^{*}(1-a)f'(E^{*})]E^{*} - (b + g_{H}^{*})H^{*}\right\}.$$

Some algebra leads to:

$$a\left[f'(E^{*})[g_{H}^{*}(Y_{m}^{*} - 1)E^{*}H^{*} - g_{m}^{*}(Y_{H}^{*} - 1)E^{*}m^{*}\right] - f'(E^{*})[g_{H}^{*} + bY_{m}^{*}]E^{*}H^{*} -$$
$$-bg_{m}^{*}m^{*}H^{*}.$$

The sign of the above expression depends, in particular, on the values of parameters a and b and of the partial derivatives involved.

Coefficient a_0 corresponds to the negative value of the determinant of the *Jacobian* matrix:

$$\begin{aligned} a_0 &= [F_{12}^* (F_{21}^* F_{33}^* - F_{23}^* F_{31}^*) + F_{13}^* (F_{22}^* F_{31}^* - F_{21}^* F_{32}^*)] = \\ &= -af'(E^*)m^* \left[g_m^* (Y_H^* - 1)(b + g_H^*) E^* H^* + g_m^* [bY_m^* - Y_H^* (b + g_H^*) + g_H^*] E^* H^* \right] + \\ &\quad + bm^* \left[g_m^* a Y_m^* f'(E^*) E^* H^* + g_m^* (1-a) Y_H^* f'(E^*) E^* H^* - g_m^* (Y_H^* - 1)(1-a) f'(E^*) E^* H^* \right]. \end{aligned}$$

By rearranging terms and with some algebra the formula above is reduced to the following positive expression:

$$a_0 = bg_m^* f'(E^*) m^* E^* H^*.$$

Finally, condition (*iv*) of the Routh-Hurwicz criterion, i.e. $[a_1 a_2 - a_0]$, is given by:

$$\begin{aligned} &\left[af'(E^*)(Y_m^* - Y_H^*) E^* + f'(E^*) Y_H^* E^* + (b + g_H^*) H^* \right] \cdot \\ &\cdot \left\{ a \left(f'(E^*) [g_H^* (Y_m^* - 1) E^* H^* - g_m^* (Y_H^* - 1) E^* m^* \right) + f'(E^*)(g_H^* + bY_m^*) E^* H^* + bg_m^* m^* H^* \right\} - \\ &- \left[bg_m^* f'(E^*) m^* E^* H^* \right]. \end{aligned}$$

Its sign depends on the values of parameters a and b, in particular, and of the partial derivatives involved.

Therefore, the following signs for the conditions (*i*)-(*iv*) are obtained:

$$a_2 = -[\underset{(-)}{F_{22}^*} + \underset{(-)}{F_{33}^*}] > 0,$$

$$a_1 = [\underset{(-)}{F^*_{22}}\,\underset{(-)}{F^*_{33}} - \underset{(-)}{F^*_{32}}\,\underset{(-)}{F^*_{23}}] + [-\underset{(-)}{F^*_{31}}\,\underset{(+)}{F^*_{13}}] + [-\underset{(-)}{F^*_{12}}\,\underset{(-)}{F^*_{21}}] \gtreqless 0,$$

$$a_0 = [F^*_{12}(F^*_{21}F^*_{33} - F^*_{23}F^*_{31}) + F^*_{13}(F^*_{22}F^*_{31} - F^*_{21}F^*_{32})] > 0,$$

$$[a_1 a_2 - a_0] \gtreqless 0.$$

Under the assumptions made at [B.3] stability depends on the signs of (*ii*) and (*iv*). In particular, with regard to condition (*ii*), relatively small values of $(F^*_{23}F^*_{32})$ and $(F^*_{21}F^*_{12})$ yield $a_1 > 0$.

More generally, the nature of the equilibrium solution and the dynamic behaviour of the model depend on the parameters which appear in system [S1], since they influence the (steady-state) equilibrium solution and the *Jacobian*, thus determining the signs of conditions (*ii*) and (*iv*). As one or more parameters change a qualitative change in the behaviour of the system may take place: this change may be the source of a *bifurcation*.

In order to study the *Hopf* bifurcations which imply the emergence of closed orbits in a system that has only one fixed point, the following theorem may be employed[3]:

Consider the differential equation system:

$$\dot{\mathbf{x}} = f(\mathbf{x}, \mu), \quad \mathbf{x} \in \mathbf{A} \subset \Re^n, \quad \mu \in \Re \;, \qquad \text{[T.1]}$$

where $\mathbf{x}$ is the vector of the state variables and μ denotes an exogenously given parameter. Assume that for each μ the system posses a unique fixed point, indicated as x^*:

3 This is a reduced form of J. Guckeinheimer – P. Holmes (1983), p. 151 ff., given in G. Gabisch –H.W. Lorenz (1989), p. 163. Cf. also G. Gandolfo (1996).

$\dot{\mathbf{x}} = \mathbf{0} = f(x^*, \mu)$.

By the implicit function theorem, if the determinant of the *Jacobian* does not vanish, then, $x^* = x^*(\mu)$.

The *Hopf* theorem is here summarised[4].

Suppose that system [T.1] posses a unique equilibrium (x^*, μ), at which the following properties are satisfied:

(i): the *Jacobian* of [T.1] has a pair of pure imaginary eigenvalues and no other eigenvalues with zero real part.

This implies that there is a smooth curve of equilibria $(x^*(\mu), \mu)$ with $x^*(\mu_0) = x^*$. The complex eigenvalues of the Jacobian $\lambda(\mu)$, $\bar{\lambda}(\mu)$ which are purely imaginary at $\mu = \mu_0$ vary smoothly with μ. If, moreover:

$$\text{(ii)}: \frac{d(\mathrm{Re}\,\lambda(\mu)}{d\mu}_{|\mu=\mu_0} > 0,$$

then, at $x^*(\mu_0)$ there is a bifurcation with periodic solutions, and the period is approximately $2\pi / \beta_0 (\beta_0 = \lambda(\mu_0)/i)$.

This implies that the formerly stable fixed point $x^*(\mu)$ loses its stability at $\mu = \mu_0$ as parameter μ is increased, since the real parts (Re λ) become positive after having crossed the imaginary axis.

In short terms, in order to verify the existence of closed orbits, it is necessary to check that by increasing the control parameter μ the following

4 This is the "existence" part of the theorem, stating the sufficient conditions for the emergence of closed orbits; the "stability" part, showing the sufficient conditions for the stability of closed orbits is rather analytically complicate, and it appears quite difficult to understand the economic meaning of the resulting conditions.

conditions are satisfied: conjugated complex roots emerge, or exist; at the bifurcation point $\mu = \mu_0$ the real parts of a pair of purely imaginary roots vanish; all the remaining real roots are different from zero at $\mu = \mu_0$; the real parts of the conjugated complex roots are different from zero at $\mu > \mu_0$.

In Section B.3 a numerical illustration is presented in which the behaviour of the model is examined as some of the parameters on which it depends are changed.

B.3 – A Numerical Illustration

Here is a numerical illustration of the behaviour of model I, in its simple form considered in this Appendix, when parameter *a* is changed.

Let the following be the values of the coefficients in the IS and LM equations of system [B.2]:

$$s = 0.75; g = 0.45; h_0 = 0.65; h_1 = 0.1; A = 0.025,$$

and, with regard to the remaining coefficients of the dynamic model, set:

$$a = 0.1; b = 0.2;$$
$$n = 0.015; \lambda = 0.025; \mu = 0.05;$$
$$\gamma = 0.2613; \psi = 0.31, \overline{H} = 0.205$$

where γ and ψ are the coefficients of the Phillips curve, that is, of function $f(E)$, which is assumed to be of a linear form as follows:

$$f(E) = -\gamma + \psi(E).$$

The steady-state solution to system [S1] is obtained by solving the following system:

$$\begin{bmatrix} \dot{m} \\ \dot{E} \\ \dot{H} \end{bmatrix} = \mathbf{0}$$

It, then, follows:

$$\begin{cases} E = \dfrac{\lambda + \gamma}{\psi} + \dfrac{b/a}{\psi}(H - \overline{H}) \\ g[m, H] = n + \lambda \\ \mu - \dfrac{b}{a}(H - \overline{H}) = g[m, H] \end{cases} \qquad \text{[E*]}$$

which may also be written as:

$$\begin{cases} H = \dfrac{\mu - (n + \lambda)}{b/a} + \overline{H} \\ E = \dfrac{\lambda + \gamma}{\psi} + \dfrac{\mu - (n + \lambda)}{\psi} \\ m = (n + \lambda)g^{-1} \end{cases}$$

Let equation [B.1], which was given in Appendix B.1, be the specification adopted for $I/K = g[m, H]$. Then, with some calculations the explicit form of function g in terms of m and H is easily obtained:

$$g[m,H] = \frac{(1-1/m)[sh_1 A + sgH]}{(1-1/m)(s-g)h_1 + gh_0},$$

which can be solved for *m*, into the third equation of system [E*]. In order to obtain the stationary solution of the system, substitute for the corresponding values of the coefficients. This gives:

m^*=1.19439; E^*=0.956452; H^*=0.21;

Therefore, the steady-state values for the profit-share, the wage-share and the output/capital ratio may be calculated (approximately):

$\Pi/X = (1\text{-}1/m) = 0.1627$; $W/X = (1/m) = 0.8837$;

$X/K = y = 0.3276$.

It is now possible to calculate the following partial derivatives – evaluated at the equilibrium point[5]:

$$Y^*_m = -0.034;\ Y^*_H = 1.5008;\ g^*_m = 0.726;\ g^*_H = 0.183.$$

On the basis of these values the *Jacobian* is calculated. For $a = 0.1$ the characteristic equation associated with the system has one negative real root (λ_1) and two conjugated complex roots (λ_2 and λ_3) with negative real part:

$$\lambda_1 = -0.458202;\ \lambda_{2,3} = -0.0105991 \pm 0.153445i,\quad i \equiv \sqrt{-1}.$$

By increasing parameter *a*, and leaving the remaining coefficients unchanged, at $a = a_0$ (which in this case of the numerical example is slightly

5 See Appendix B.1. All values are approximated.

above 0.1) the system loses stability. The real parts of the conjugated complex roots become positive, after having crossed the imaginary axis. Moreover, at the bifurcation point the remaining root is different from zero.

For instance, if $a = 0.2$ the following results are obtained:

m^*=1.18909; E^*=0.956425; H^*=0.215.

$\Pi/X = (1\text{-}1/m) = 0.159$; $W/X = (1/m) = 0.841$;

$X/K = y = 0.335$.

$Y^*_m = -0.03557$; $Y^*_H = 1.5017$; $g^*_m = 0.722$; $g^*_H = 0.179$;

and the eigenvalues of the system are:

$$\lambda_1 = -0.447283; \quad \lambda_{2,3} = 0.00499157 \pm 0.156989i, \quad i \equiv \sqrt{-1}.$$

Therefore, the sufficient conditions of the *Hopf* theorem for the existence of closed orbits, which were given in Section B.2, appear to be satisfied.

Notice that parameter b acts in the opposite direction to parameter a: for higher values of b the bifurcation point of a is also higher. For instance, in the example above, if $b = 0.3$, then the bifurcation point of a is slightly above 0.2.

B.4 – A Brief Note on Monetary Policy

If a counter-cyclical monetary policy rule is adopted[6], and equation [P.1] is added to the constant and exogenously determined quantity μ, then system [S1] is turned into the following fundamental system:

---

6 See Chapter III.

[P1*]=

$$\dot{m} = \{-a[f(E)-\lambda]+b(H-\overline{H}\}\, m \equiv F_1(m,E,H);$$

$$\dot{E} = \{\, Y_m[-a[f(E)-\lambda]+b(H-\overline{H})]+$$
$$+Y_H[[\mu+\delta(m-\overline{m})+\theta(E-\overline{E})]-(1-a)[f(E)-\lambda]-b(H-\overline{H})-g(m,H)]+$$
$$+g(m,H)-(n+\lambda)\,\}E \equiv F_2(m,E,H);$$

$$\dot{H} = \{[\mu+\delta(m-\overline{m})+\theta(E-\overline{E})]-(1-a)[f(E)-\lambda]-b(H-\overline{H})-g(m,H)\}H \equiv$$
$$\equiv F_3(m,E,H).$$

At this point, the analysis can be carried out by proceeding as in the previous section. Once again, the linearisation of system [P1*] around the equilibrium point makes it possible to have information on the "local" behaviour of the system.

Now, the *Jacobian* of the system is clearly different, and consequently the nature of the solutions is different too. In particular, for given values of parameters a and b, there exist a range of values for the monetary policy parameters δ and θ within which the system is stable, whereas it would be unstable with a fixed monetary policy rule. To see this in more detail, the elements in the *Jacobian* matrix associated with system [P1*] have to be calculated. In the presence of a counter-cyclical monetary policy, with δ and θ as policy parameters, they are the following:

$$F^*_{11} = 0\,;$$

$$F^*_{12} = -\,a\,f'(E^*)\,m^*;$$

$$F^*_{13} = b\,m^*;$$

$$F^*_{21} = \{Y^*_H[(-g^*_m)+\delta]+g^*_m\}E^* \;=\; \{-g^*_m(Y^*_H-1)+Y^*_H\delta\}E^*;$$

$$F^*_{22} = \{Y^*_m(-a)f'(E^*)-Y^*_H[(1-a)f'(E^*)-\theta]\}\;E^*\,;$$

$$F_{23}^* = \{Y_m^* b - Y_H^* (b + g_H^*) + g_H^*\} E^* = \{b(Y_m^* - Y_H^*) - g_H^* (Y_H^* - 1)\} E^*;$$

$$F_{31}^* = \{-g_m^* + \delta\} H^*;$$

$$F_{32}^* = \{-(1-a) f'(E^*) - \theta\} H^*;$$

$$F_{33}^* = \{-(b + g_H^*)\} H^*.$$

It is possible to prove that if the system is unstable at a given value of parameter a, and with a constant monetary policy rule, that is, with $\delta = \theta = 0$, then by choosing an appropriate active policy rule stability may be increased.

In the example of Section B.3, the system is unstable for $a > 0.15$, with $\delta = \theta = 0$. If an active policy is adopted instead, then by choosing, for instance, $\delta = \theta = 1.5$ as policy parameters, the roots of the characteristic equation will all have negative real part:

$$\lambda_1 = -2.54024; \quad \lambda_{2,3} = -0.0247729 \pm 0.329061 i, \quad i \equiv \sqrt{-1}.$$

B.5 – Notes on the Dynamics of the Enlarged Model

The analysis can be performed as in the previous sections in order to have information on the "local" behaviour of the model in the neighbourhood of the fixed point. After having determined the stationary solution to system [S2], the elements of matrix J associated with the linearised system can be calculated[7]:

$$F_{11}^* = 0;$$

7 See Chapter IV.

$$F_{12}^{*} = -\, a f'(E^{*})\, m^{*};$$

$$F_{13}^{*} = b\, m^{*};$$

$$F_{21}^{*} = \{Y_{\Theta}^{*}[(-g_{m}^{*}) + \phi_1 r_{m}^{*}] + g_{m}^{*}\}E^{*} \;=\; \{-g_{m}^{*}(Y_{\Theta}^{*} - 1) + Y_{\Theta}^{*}\phi_1 r_{m}^{*}\}E^{*};$$

$$F_{22}^{*} = \{Y_{m}^{*}(-a) f'(E^{*}) - Y_{\Theta}^{*}[(1-a) f'(E^{*})]\}\; E^{*};$$

$$F_{23}^{*} = \{Y_{m}^{*} b - Y_{\Theta}^{*}[(b + g_{\Theta}^{*}) + (\phi_1 r_{\Theta}^{*} - \phi_2)] + g_{\Theta}^{*}\}E^{*} = \\ = \{b(Y_{m}^{*} - Y_{\Theta}^{*}) - g_{\Theta}^{*}(Y_{\Theta}^{*} - 1) + Y_{\Theta}^{*}(\phi_1 r_{m}^{*} - \phi_2)\}E^{*};$$

$$F_{31}^{*} = \{-g_{m}^{*} + \phi_1 r_{m}^{*}\}\Theta^{*};$$

$$F_{32}^{*} = \{-(1-a) f'(E^{*})\}\Theta^{*};$$

$$F_{33}^{*} = \{-(b + g_{H}^{*}) + (\phi_1 r_{M}^{*} - \phi_2\}\Theta^{*},$$

where coefficients ϕ_1 and ϕ_2 measure the sensitivity of the growth rate of money, in nominal terms, to the rate of profit (r = (1-1/m)y) and to the total stock of money in real terms (Θ), respectively.

In the example of Section B.3, with a = 0.2, if $\phi_1 = 1.5$ and $\phi_2 = 1.8$ all eigenvalues have negative real part, and so liquidity acts as a stabilising factor; if ϕ_1 is relatively small (for instance, $\phi_1 = 1$; $\phi_2 = 1.8$), or if ϕ_2 is relatively large then there are two conjugate complex roots with positive real part and this indicates that the system is unstable. In this case, liquidity acts as a destabilising factor.

REFERENCES

ALLEN, R. G. D. (1963) - *Mathematical Economics*. London: Macmillan.

ASADA, T. (1989) - "Monetary Stabilisation Policy in a Keynes-Goodwin Model of The Growth Cycle". In Semmler, W. (1989), pp. 145-167.

ASADA, T. (1994) – "Monetary Factors and Gestation Lag in a Kaleckian Model of the Business Cycle". In Semmler, W. (1994), pp. 289-310.

BAUMOL, W. J. (1958) - "Topology of Second Order Linear Difference Equations with Constant Coefficients". *Econometrica*, 26, pp. 258-285.

BAUMOL, W. J. (1970) – *Economic Dynamics*, 3rd edition. New York: MacMillan.

BELTRAMI, E. (1987) - *Mathematics for Dynamic Modelling*. New York: Academic Press.

BENHABIB, J. (ed.) (1992) – *Cycles and Chaos in Economic Equilibrium*. Princeton: Princeton University Press.

BENHABIB, J. and DAY, R. H. (1982) - "A Characterization of Erratic Dynamics in the Overlapping Generations Model". *Journal of Economics Dynamics and Control*, 48, pp. 459-472.

BERNARKE, B. S. (1983) – "Non-monetary Effects of the Financial Crises in the Propagation of the Great Depression". *American Economic Review*, 73, pp. 257-276.

BERNANKE, B. S. and GERTLER, M. (1987) - "Banking and Macroeconomic Equilibrium". In Barnett, W. and Singleton, K. (eds.): *New Approaches to Monetary Economics*. New York: Cambridge University Press.

BERNANKE, B. S. and GERTLER, M. (1990) - "Financial Fragility and Economic Performance". *Quarterly Journal of Economics*, 105, pp. 87-114.

BERNANKE, B. S. and GERTLER, M. (1989) – "Agency Costs, Net Worth and Business Fluctuations". *American Economic Review*, 79, pp. 14-31.

BLANCHARD, O. and FISHER, S. (1989) - *Lectures on Macroeconomics*. Cambridge: MIT Press.

BLINDER, A. and STIGLITZ, J. E. (1983) - "Money, Credit Constraints and Economic Activity". *American Economic Review*, 73, pp. 297-302.

BURNS, A. F. and MITCHELL, W. C. (1946) - *Measuring Business Cycles. Studies in Business Cycles*. No.2. New York: NBER.

CALOMIRIS, C. W. and HUBBARD, R. G. (1990) - "Firm Heterogeneity, Internal Finance and Credit Rationing". *Economic Journal*, 100, pp. 90-104.

CHANG, W. W. and SMITH, D. J. (1971) - "The Existence and Persistence of Cycles in a Nonlinear Model: Kaldor's 1940 Model Re-examined". *Review of Economic Studies*, 38, pp. 37-44.

DAY, R. H. (1994) – *Complex Economic Dynamics*. Vol. 1. London: The MIT Press.

DELLI GATTI, D. and GALLEGATI, M. (1994) - "External Finance, Investment Expenditure and the Business Cycle". In Semmler, W. (1994), pp. 269-288.

DELLI GATTI, D., GALLEGATI, M. and GARDINI, L. (1993) - "Investment Confidence, Corporate Debt and Income Fluctuations". *Journal of Economic Behaviour and Organization*, 22, pp. 161-187.

DESAI, M. (1973) - "Growth Cycles and Inflation in a Model of Class Struggle". *Journal of Economic Theory*, 6, pp. 527-545.

DI MATTEO, M. (1984) - "Alternative Monetary Policies in a Classical Growth Cycle". In Goodwin, R. M., Krüger, M. and Vercelli, A. (1984), pp. 14-24.

DOMAR, E. D. (1946) - "Capital Expansion, Rate of Growth and Employment". *Econometrica*, 14, pp. 137-142.

DOMAR, E. D. (1947) – "Expansion and Employment". *American Economic Review*, 37, pp. 34-55.

DOMAR, E. D. (1957) - *Essays in the Theory of Economic Growth*. New York: Oxford University Press.

DORE, M. H. I. (1993) - *The Macrodynamics of Business Cycles. A Comparative Evaluation*. Cambridge MA & Oxford UK: Basil Blackwell.

ECKSTEIN, O. and SINAI, A. (1986) - "The Mechanism of the Business Cycle in the Post-war Era". In Gordon, R. J. (1986), pp. 39-105.

FAZZARI, S., HUBBARD, G. and PETERSEN, B. (1988) - "Financing Constraints and Corporate Investment". *Brooking Papers on Economic Activity*, 1, pp. 141-206.

FISHER, I. (1933) - "The Debt Deflation Theory of Great Depression". *Econometrica*, 1, pp. 337-357.

FLASCHEL, P. (1984) – "Some Stability Properties of Goodwin's Growth Cycle. A Critical Elaboration". *Zeitschrift für Nationalökonomie*, 44, pp. 63-69.

FLASCHEL, P. (1984a) "The Inflation-Based 'Natural' Rate of Unemployment and the Conflict over Income Distribution". In Goodwin, R. M., Krüger, M. and Vercelli, A. (1984), pp. 103-126.

FOLEY, D. (1986) - "Stabilization Policy in a Nonlinear Business Cycle Model". In Semmler, W. (ed.): *Competition, Instability, and Nonlinear*

Cycles. Lecture Notes in Economics and Mathematical Systems. Heidelberg and New York: Springer-Verlag, pp. 200-211.

FOLEY, D. (1987) - "Liquidity-Profit Rate Cycles in a Capitalist Economy". *Journal of Economic Behaviour and Organization*, 8, pp. 363-377.

FRANKE, R. and SEMMLER, W. (1989) - "Debt Financing of Firms, Stability and Cycles in a Dynamical Macroeconomic Growth Model". In Semmler, W. (1989), pp. 38-64.

FRANKE, R. and SEMMLER, W. (1994) – "A Model of the Financial Sector and Its Reaction to Aggregate Fluctuations". In Semmler, W. (1994), pp. 231-268.

FRIEDMAN, B. M. (1980) – "Post-war Changes in the American Financial Markets", in Feldstein, M. (ed.): *The American Economy Transition*. Chicago: University of Chicago Press, pp. 9-78.

FRIEDMAN, B. M. (1982) – *The Changing Role of Debt and Equity in Financing U.S. Capital Formation*. Chicago: University of Chicago Press.

FRISCH, R. (1933) – "Propagation Problems and Impulse Problems in Dynamic Economics", in *Essays in Honour of Gustav Cassel*. London: Allen & Unwin, pp. 171-205.

GABISCH, G. and LORENZ, H. W. (1989) - *Business Cycles: A Survey of Methods and Concepts*. 2nd Edition. Heidelberg - New York: Springer-Verlag.

GALLEGATI, M. and GARDINI, L. (1991) - "A Nonlinear Model of the Business Cycle with Money and Finance". *Metroeconomica*, 42, pp. 1-32.

GANDOLFO, G. (1996) - *Economic Dynamics*. Complete, Revised and Enlarged Edition. Heidelberg and New York: Springer-Verlag.

GERTLER, M. (1988) - "Financial Structure and Aggregate Economic Activity". *Journal of Money, Credit and Banking*, 20, pp. 559-588.

GLASNER, D. (1993) - *Encyclopedia of Business Cycles, Panics, Crises and Depressions*. New York: Garland Publishing.

GOODWIN, R. M. (1948) – "Secular and Cyclical Aspects of the Multiplier and Accelerator". In *Employment, Income and Public Policy*. Essays in Honour of A. H. Hansen. New York: W. Norton.

GOODWIN, R. M. (1951) - "The Nonlinear Acceleration and the Persistence of Business Cycles". *Econometrica*, 19, pp. 1-17.

GOODWIN, R. M. (1967) - "A Growth Cycle". In Feinstein, C. H. (ed.): *Socialism, Capitalism and Economic Growth.* Essays Presented to Maurice Dobb. Cambridge: Cambridge University Press, pp. 54-58.

GOODWIN, R. M., KRÜGER, M. and VERCELLI, A. (eds.) (1984) - *Nonlinear Models of Fluctuating Growth.* Lecture Notes in Economics and Mathematical Systems. Heidelberg and New York: Springer-Verlag.

GORDON, R. J. (ed.) (1986) - *The American Business Cycle.* Chicago: University of Chicago Press.

GRANDMONT, J. M. (1985) - "On Endogenous Competitive Business Cycles". *Econometrica*, 5, pp. 995-1045.

GRAZIANI, A. (1984) - "The Debate on Keynes' Finance Motive". *Economic Notes*, 1, pp. 5-34.

GREENWALD, B. and STIGLITZ, J. E. (1986) - "Externalities in Economies with Imperfect Information and Incomplete Markets". *Quarterly Journal of Economics*, 105, pp. 87-114.

GREENWALD, B. and STIGLITZ, J. E. (1990) - "Macroeconomic Models with Equity and Credit Rationing". In Hubbard, R. G. (ed.): *Asymmetric Information, Corporate Finance and Investment.* Chicago: University of Chicago Press.

GREENWALD, B. and STIGLITZ, J. E. (1993) – "Financial Market Imperfections and Business Cycles". *Quarterly Journal of Economics*, 108, pp. 77-114.

GREENWALD, B., STIGLITZ, J. E. and WEISS, A. (1984) - "Informational Imperfections in the Capital Market and Macroeconomic Fluctuations". *American Economic Review*, 74, pp. 194-200.

GUCKENHEIMER, J. and HOLMES, P. (1983) - *Nonlinear Oscillations, Dynamical Systems and Bifurcations of Vector Fields*. Heidelberg and New York: Springer-Verlag.

GURLEY, J. and SHAW, E. (1955) - "Financial Aspects of Economic Development". *American Economic Review*, 45, pp. 515-538.

GURLEY, J. and SHAW, E. (1960) - *Money in a Theory of Finance*. Washington: Brookings Institutions.

HARROD, R. F. (1939) - " An Essay in Dynamic Theory". *Economic Journal*, 49, pp. 14-33.

HARROD, R. F. (1948) - *Towards a Dynamic Economics*. London: Macmillan.

HICKS, J. R. (1950) - *A Contribution to the Theory of Trade Cycle*. Oxford: Oxford University Press.

HIRSCH, M. W. and SMALE, S. (1974) - *Differential Equations, Dynamical Systems, and Linear Algebra*. New York: Academic Press.

JUGLAR, C. (1862) – *Des Crises Commerciales et de leur Retour Périodique en France, en Angleterre et aux Etats Unis*. Paris: Guillaumin.

KALDOR, M. (1940) - "A Model of the Trade Cycle". *Económic Journal*, 50, pp. 78-92.

KALECKI, M. (1935) - "A Macroeconomic Theory of the Business Cycle". *Econometrica*, 3, pp. 327-344.

KALECKI, M. (1937) - "A Theory of the Business Cycle". *Review of Economic Studies*, 4, pp. 77-97.

KALECKI, M. (1937a) - "The Principle of Increasing Risk". *Economica*, 4, pp. 440-447.

KALECKI, M. (1939) - "A Theory of the Business Cycle". In Kalecki, M. (1972), pp. 116-149.

KALECKI, M. (1943) - *Studies in Economic Dynamics*. London: Allen & Unwin.

KALECKI, M. (1954) - *Theory of Economic Dynamics*. London: Allen & Unwin.

KALECKI, M. (1971) - *Selected Essays on the Dynamics of the Capitalist Economy*. Cambridge: Cambridge University Press.

KALECKI, M. (1972) - *Essays in the Theory of Economic Fluctuations*. London: Allen & Unwin.

KEYNES, J. M. (1936) - *The General Theory of Employment, Interest and Money*. London: MacMillan.

KEYNES, J. M. - *The Collected Writings of John Maynard Keynes*. Voll. XIII and XIV (1973), Vol. XXIX (1979). London: MacMillan.

KITCHIN, J. (1923) – "Cycles and Trends in Economic Factors". *Review of Economic Statistics*, 5, pp. 10-16.

KONDRATIEFF, N. D. (1932) – "The Long Waves in Economic Life". *Review of Economic Statistics*, 17, pp. 105-115.

KYDLAND, F. and PRESCOTT, E. F. (1982) - "Time to Build and Aggregate Fluctuations". *Econometrica*, 50, pp. 1345-1370.

KUTZNETS, S. (1971) – *Economic Growth of Nations*. Cambridge: Belknap Press of Harvard University Press.

LASOTA, A. and MACKEY, M. (1985) - *Probabilistic Properties of Deterministic Systems*. Cambridge: Cambridge University Press.

LI, T. Y. and YORKE, J. (1975) - "Period Three Implies Chaos". *American Mathematical Monthly*, 82, pp. 985-992.

LIENARD, A. (1928) – "Etude des Oscillations Entretenues". *Revue Generale de l'Electricite*, 23, pp. 901-946.

LONG, J. B. and PLOSSER, C. I. (1983) - "Real Business Cycle". *Journal of Political Economy*, 91, pp. 39-69.

LOTKA, A. Y. (1925) - *Elements of Physical Biology*. Baltimore: Wiliams & Wilkens.

LUCAS, R. E. (1975) - "An Equilibrium Model of the Business Cycle". In Lucas, R. E. (1981), pp. 179-214.

LUCAS, R. E. (1981) – *Studies in Business Cycle Theory*. Cambridge: The MIT Press.

MANKIW, N. G. (1989) - "Real Business Cycle: A New Keynesian Perspective". *Journal of Economic Perspectives*, 3, pp. 79-90.

MANKIW, N. G. and ROMER, D. (eds) (1991) - *New Keynesian Economics*. Vols. I-II. Cambridge: The MIT Press.

MARX, K. (1967) – *Capital*. Vol. 1. New York: International Publishers.

MEDIO, A. (1979) - *Teoria nonlineare del ciclo economico*. Bologna: Il Mulino.

MINSKY, H. P. (1975) - *John Maynard Keynes*. New York: Columbia University Press.

MINSKY, H. P. (1982) - *Can "It" Happen Again? Essays on Instability and Finance*. New York and London: M. E. Sharpe, Inc.

MISHKIN, F. (1978) - "The Household Balance Sheet in the Great Depression". *Journal of Economic History*, 38, pp. 918-937.

MITCHELL, W. C. (1927) - *Business Cycles: The Problem and its Setting*. New York: NBER.

MODIGLIANI, F. and MILLER, M. (1958) – "The Cost of Capital, Corporation Finance and the Theory of Investment". *American Economic Review*, 48, pp. 261-297.

MOORE, G. H. (1961) - *Business Cycle Indicators*. Vol.1. Princeton: Princeton University Press.

MOORE, G. H. and ZARNOVITZ, V. (1986) - "Appendix A. The Development and Role of the NBER's Business Cycle Chronologies". In Gordon, R. J. (1986), pp. 735-779.

NIGGLE, C. J. (1989) - "The Cyclical Behaviour of Corporate Financial Ratios and Minsky's Financial Instability Hypothesis". In Semmler, W. (1989), pp. 203-220.

PASINETTI, L. L. (1960) – "Cyclical Fluctuations and Growth". *Oxford Economic Papers,* 12, pp. 215-241.

PHILLIPS, A. W. H. (1958) – "The Relation between Unemployment and Rate of Change of Money Wage Rates in the United Kingdom, 1861-1958". *Economica*, 25, pp. 283-299.

RICARDO, D. (1817) – *The Principles of Political Economy and Taxation*. London: Dent and Son Ltd. (1960).

RODANO, G. (1996) - *Lezioni sulle teorie del ciclo*. Manuscript.

RUELLE, D. and TAKENS, F. (1971) - "On the Nature of Turbulence, Communications". *Mathematical Physics*, 20, pp. 176-192.

SAMUELSON, P. A. (1939) – "Interactions Between the Multiplier Analysis and the Principle of Acceleration". *Review of Economic Studies*, 21, pp. 75-78.

SARGENT, T. (1987) – *Macroeconomic Theory*. 2nd Edition. New York: Academic Press.

SCHUMPETER, J. A. (1911) - *The Theory of Economic Development*. New York: Oxford University Press.

SCHUMPETER, J. A. (1928) - "The Instability of Capitalism". *The Economic Journal*, 38, pp. 361-386.

SCHUMPETER, J. A. (1939) - *Business Cycles*. New York: McGraw-Hill.

SEMMLER, W. (ed.) (1988) - *Financial Dynamics and Business Cycles: New Perspectives*. New York and London: M. E. Sharpe, Inc.

SEMMLER, W. (ed.) (1994) - *Business Cycles: Theory and Empirical Methods*. Boston and London: Kluwer Publishers.

SEMMLER, W. and SIEVEKING, M. (1993) - "Nonlinear Liquidity-Growth Dynamics with Corridor Stability". *Journal of Economic Behaviour and Organization*, 22, pp. 189-208.

SIMMONS, G. F. (1972) - *Differential Equations: with Applications and Historical Notes*. New York: McGraw-Hill. (Also published as Simmons, G. F. (1974). New Delhi: Tata McGraw-Hill).

SLUTSKY, E. (1927) - *The Summation of Random Causes as the Source of Cyclic Processes*. 3, n.1, Moscow: Conjuncture Institute.

SMITH, A. (1776) – *The Wealth of Nations*. London: Dent and Son Ltd. (1964).

SORDI, S. (1990) - *Teorie del ciclo economico*. Bologna: ed. CLUEB.

STEINDL, V. J. (1981) – "Some Comments on the Three Versions of Kalecki's Theory of the Trade Cycle". In Los, J. et al. (eds.), *Studies in Economic*

Theory and Practise. Essays in Honour of Edward Lipinsky. Amsterdam: North Holland.

STIGLITZ, J. E. (1992) - "Capital Markets and Economic Fluctuations in Capitalist Economies". *European Economic Review*, 36, pp. 269-306.

STIGLITZ, J. E. and WEISS, A. (1981) - "Credit Rationing in Markets with Imperfect Information". *American Economic Review*, 71, pp. 393-410.

SYLOS LABINI, P. (1967) - "Prezzi, distribuzione e investimenti in Italia dal 1951 al 1966: uno schema interpretativo". *Moneta e Credito*, 20, pp. 265-344.

SYLOS LABINI, P. (1970) – *Problemi dello sviluppo economico*. Bari: Editori Laterza.

SYLOS LABINI, P. (1993) - *Economic Growth and Business Cycles: Prices and the Process of Cyclical Development*. Aldershot: E. Elgar.

SUMMERS, L. H. (1986) - "Some Sceptical Observations on Real Business Cycle Theory". *Quarterly Review Federal Reserve Bank of Minneapolis*, 10, pp. 23-27.

TAKAYAMA, A. (1974) – *Mathematical Economics*. Hinsdale Ill.: The Dryden Press.

TAYLOR, L. and O'CONNEL, S. A. (1985) - "A Minsky Crisis". *Quarterly Journal of Economics*, 100, pp. 871-886.

THIO, K. B. T. (1984) - "Cyclical and Structural Aspects of Unemployment and Growth in a Nonlinear Model of Cyclical Growth". In Goodwin, R. M., Krüger, M. and Vercelli, A. (1984), pp. 127-145.

THOM, R. (1977) – "What is Catastrophe Theory about". In Hacken, H. (ed): *Synergetics. A Workshop*. Heidelberg and New York: Springer-Verlag.

THOM, R. (1980) - *Parabole e catastrofi*. Milano: Il Saggiatore.

VACIAGO, G. (1987) - *Teoria e politica monetaria*. Bologna: Il Mulino.

VELUPILLAI, K. (1979) - "Some Stability Properties of Goodwin's Growth Cycle Model". *Zeitschrift für Nationalökonomie*, 39, pp. 245-257.

VERCELLI, A. (1981) - "Equilibrio e disequilibrio nella Teoria Generale di Keynes". In A.A.VV., *Studi di Economia Keynesiana*. Napoli: Liguori.

VERCELLI, A. (1984) - "Fluctuations and Growth: Keynes, Schumpeter and Marx and the Stuctural Instabilty of Capitalism". In Goodwin R.M., Krüger, M. and Vercelli, A. (1984), pp. 209-231.

VICARELLI, F. (1977) - *Keynes, l'instabilità del capitalismo*. Milano: Etas.

VOLTERRA, V. (1931) - *Lecons sur la Theorie Mathematique de la Lutte pour la Vie*. Paris: Gauthier-Villars.

WOLFSON, M. H. (1989) - "Theories of Financial Crises". In Semmler, W. (1989), pp. 221-227.

WOODFORD, M. (1986) - "Stationary Sunspot Equilibria in a Finance Constrained Economy". *Journal of Economic Theory*, 40, pp. 128-137.

WOODFORD, M. (1988) - "Imperfect Financial Intermediation and Complex Dynamics". In Barnett, A., Geweke, J. and Shell, K. (eds.): *Economic Complexity: Chaos, Sunspots, Bubbles, and Nonlinearity*. Cambridge: Cambridge University Press, pp. 309-334.

WOODFORD, M. (1989) - "Finance, Instability, and Cycles". In Semmler, W. (1989), pp. 18-37.

ZARNOVITZ, V. and MOORE, G. H. (1986) – "Major Changes in Cyclical Behaviour". In Gordon, R. J. (1986), pp. 519-574.

DYNAMISCHE WIRTSCHAFTSTHEORIE

Herausgegeben von Peter Flaschel und Michael Krüger

Band 1 Reiner Franke: Production Prices and Dynamical Processes of the Gravitation of Market Prices. 1987.

Band 2 Peter Flaschel / Michael Krüger (eds.): Recent Approaches to Economic Dynamics. Conference Volume (Bielefeld: 7-9th October, 1987). 1988.

Band 3 Richard M. Goodwin: Essays in Nonlinear Economic Dynamics. Collected Papers 1980-1987. 1988.

Band 4 Peter Skott: Kaldor's Growth And Distribution Theory. 1989.

Band 5 Jobst H. Thalenhorst: Die Zeitstruktur der Produktion als Ursache ökonomischer Dynamik. 1989.

Band 6 Volker Bieta: Strategische Möglichkeiten für die Gestaltung von Zentralbankpolitiken. Eine spieltheoretische Analyse. 1990.

Band 7 Dimitrios Malliaropulos: Euromärkte und nationale Finanzmärkte. Geldmenge, Zins und Wechselkurs einer Eurowährung. Eine theoretische und empirische Analyse des Euro-DM-Marktes. 1990.

Band 8 Thomas Lux: Keynesianische Stabilisierungspolitik in Neokeynesianischen Modellen. 1990.

Band 9 Torsten Vogt: Technischer Fortschritt und Preisentwicklung. 1991.

Band 10 Marco Wilke: Corporatism and the Stability of Capitalist Democracies. 1991.

Band 11 Ingrid Kubin: Market Prices and Natural Prices. A Study in the Theory of the Classical Process of Gravitation. 1991.

Band 12 Nobuo Okishio (ed.): Business Cycles. Theories and Numerical Simulation. 1992.

Band 13 Peter Flaschel / Michael Krüger (Eds.): Nobuo Okishio. Essays on Political Economy. Collected papers. 1993.

Band 14 Martin Arnold: Wachstum und ökologisches Gleichgewicht. 1993.

Band 15 Peter Flaschel: Macrodynamics. Income Distribution, Effective Demand and Cyclical Growth. 1993.

Band 16 Boe Thio: Nonlinear Dynamics and Unemployment Theory. 1994.

Band 17 Peter Flaschel: Fixkapital und Profitabilität. Gesamt- und einzelwirtschaftliche Aspekte. 1995.

Band 18 Michael B. E. Ackermann: Die optimale Angleichung der neuen Bundesländer an die Lebensverhältnisse in Westdeutschland. 1998.

Band 19 Christoph Kind: Investitionsfinanzierung und konjunkturelle Dynamik. 1999.

Band 20 Eleonora Cavallaro: Real and Financial Dynamics in a Macroeconomic Growth Model with Endogenous Cycles. 1999.

MIX
Papier | Fördert gute Waldnutzung
FSC® C083411

Kolibri 360 GmbH
Ferdinand-Jühlke-Straße 7
99095 Erfurt, Deutschland
produktsicherheit@kolibri360.de

Druck:
CPI Druckdienstleistungen GmbH
im Auftrag der
Kolibri 360 GmbH
Ferdinand-Jühlke-Str. 7
99095 Erfurt